SPIRITUALITY 103

THE FORGIVENESS CODE

FINDING THE LIGHT IN OUR SHADOWS

Iván Figueroa-Otero, MD

CREDITS

Author: Iván Figueroa-Otero, MD
www.ivanfigueroaoteromd.com
Editor: Yasmin Rodriguez, The Writing Ghost, Inc.
www.thewritingghost.com
Cover Design: Gil Acosta Design
www.gilacosta.com
Book Production and Set Up: The Writing Ghost, Inc.

Due to the dynamic nature of the internet, any web addresses or links contained in this book may have changed since its publication and may no longer be valid. The opinions expressed in this book are exclusive to the author.
The author's purpose is only to provide general information to assist you in your search for emotional and spiritual well-being. If you choose to use the information in this book, which is your right, the author, editor and publishing team assume no responsibility for your actions.

ISBN-13: 978-0-9964666-3-9

Second edition, 2020
Part of the series:
"School of Life"

REVIEWS

"This book is a masterpiece of writing. Iván has put a lot of time into this presentation, and it is impressive. I like the modernization of the terms and analogies. What he has done is create a series of ideas to help people get in touch with themselves, decide what is of value and move towards that. It is a complete and modern spiritual path for those who are not attracted to a more traditional approach. I congratulate him."

Jhampa Shaneman
Author of Buddhist Astrology

"Dr. Iván Figueroa-Otero writes of a journey of love, compassion, and forgiveness we must all take as we truly embrace our inner Warrior of Light. It is easy to identify the 'enemies' out there, but real change will not show up [...] until we transform the 'enemy' we have created within, and often over the course of a lifetime. This is the power of forgiveness and reconciliation that Mahatma Gandhi taught us in his philosophy of nonviolence, and this is the deep lesson of forgiveness and reprogramming that Dr. Ivan Figueroa-Otero so eloquently introduces us to in Spirituality 103. [...] As we approach our inner battle with love, compassion, and forgiveness, we begin to approach others [that way], knowing they are facing their inner battles and lessons that we may or may not have already learned ourselves."

Missy Crutchfield and Melissa Turner
Founding editors, Gandhi's Be Magazine

"Dr. Ivan Figueroa-Otero wrote a personal navigation chart for the road we call life. His education as a scientist and a Buddhist allows him to translate his spiritual reflections into a popular, common language. In this, his third book on self-help, Figueroa-Otero narrates the story of the Warrior of Light and conveys within us the desire to discover our Warrior and to launch the battle against the formidable enemies attacking us from all fronts. The setting for this battle is complex, and to describe it, he uses multiple references from mythology, religion, oriental philosophies, psychology, science, and occultism. The Warrior of Light will win its internal and external battles

if it uses the most effective weapons: love, compassion, and forgiveness."

Rafael Trelles
Illustrious Puerto Rican artist

"Dr. Ivan Figueroa-Otero, while examining one of the human's most profound deficiencies: guilt, also examines (with final tests and everything) our ego's enslaving mechanism. The author performs a broad study of the subject, using familiar analogies and combining a profound sense of spiritual release and freedom - it is the culmination of three volumes of a real, practical manual for the 'School Of Life'... A true gem."

Carli Muñoz
Musician, composer

"Dr. Ivan Figueroa-Otero is unique. His understanding of human spirituality transcends the norms. Your heart will collect true gems when reading his books. Your limited beliefs will be questioned and released. In a very unusual and practical manner, combined with a sense of humor, you will learn about yourself and the universe. It will empower you in a very powerful and unique way. This book is an astonishing work. A must read."

Anita Paniagua
Entrepreneurship developer
Author of the book *EmprendeSer*

"Dr. Ivan's book does a fantastic job of helping mankind to expand consciousness and come out of the darkness into the light, where one sees that the only barriers between man and his fellow soul-travelers and inner-peace are within one's self-limiting beliefs and false perceptions of others! He conveys this premise using universal spiritual laws and their application to human's most pressing questions of "being." The book is beautifully written and vividly expressed! And his profound answers serve not only the individual but also the collective."

Amelia Kemp, Ph.D., LMHC
Psychotherapist, ordained metaphysician, and author of "From Psychotherapy to Sacretherapy® - Alternative Holistic Descriptions & Healing Processes for 170 Mental & Emotional Diagnoses Worldwide."

"Dr. Ivan Figueroa-Otero is unique. His understanding of human spirituality transcends the norms. Your heart will collect true gems when reading his books. Your limited beliefs will be questioned and released. In a very unusual and practical manner, combined with a sense of humor, you will learn about yourself and the universe. It will empower you in a very powerful and unique way. This book is an astonishing work. A must read."

Dr Antoine Chevaler, PhD, ND, HK,
International speaker, author, researcher & teacher

"The first time I read it I traveled to a world of particular and exceptional circumstances. The second time, I had to make decisions related to my character, which I sorely needed, and that I hadn't seen in my mind's mirror. The author transports us to the infinite world within ourselves and takes us on a trip through the need of self-forgiveness to understand the need to forgive others, and the implications of that action on our mental, physical, and spiritual health. You have to read it to understand and explore the world of your emotions and experiences, and to reach the place where you wish to be: your spiritual introspection."

Dr. Norman González Chacón
Natural medicine doctor, father of the natural medicine movement in Puerto Rico

"This book and the two previous ones show that he [Dr. Ivan Figueroa-Otero] is one of those rare intellectuals who, just by studying humanity, almost covers all types of knowledge, from the *corpus Universalis* to an understanding of the human spirit. Spirituality 103 reflects a hybrid vision of occidental scientific knowledge and oriental arts and wisdom. The Epilogue is a gem of inspiration and creativity."

Dr. Eduardo Santiago-Delpín
Transplant surgeon and Immunologist,
distinguished Professor,
University Of Puerto Rico

"This book by Dr. Ivan Figueroa-Otero doesn't only reflect his own life's transition but contains an efficient formula to reach the most pristine and full integration of humans with complete and long-lasting happiness. It highlights an elaborate and elegant synthesis between different fields of knowledge such as psychology, psychiatry, genetics, spirituality, and philosophy. The book offers us methods and logical strategies to maximize our capacity for introspection, teaching us to maintain a crucial balance between the experience of life and its periodic examination, which in turn leads us to enjoy better health of mind. It frees us from ancient paradigms and conceptual limitations that cause anguish, and that so often push us to the emptiness of our alienation."

Dr. Víctor Lladó

Doctor in psychiatry

OTHER BOOKS BY THIS AUTHOR

Spirituality 101

For the Dropouts of the School of Life

A Review for the Final Exam

Spirituality 1.2

For the Disconnected from the School of Life

A Review for Tekkies

Spirituality 104

Reflections in my Magical Mirror

Lessons of Love from the School of Life

DEDICATION

I dedicate this book to all teachers, students, and patients who participate with me in the School of Life, and who inspired me to share all of their experiences and lessons. Especially my patients who, with the testimonials of their lessons of love, helped me find the Key to Forgiveness to reach the healing code of the soul. Without them, my academic progress in the universal classroom would not have been possible. If, while being reflected by this book's mirror, some of you rediscover your shadow-distorted light, share the merit of the results with your fellow students, as well as the learning that follows from reading it.

Table of Contents

ACKNOWLEDGMENTS

Among all the travelers that have shared this endless journey in the reflection of my Mind's Magical Mirror, I want to particularly thank my children, their mother and my patient wife Ivette, who have supported this old man's follies with so much affection.

I especially appreciate the spiritual guidance from my Masters in the Nyingma Tibetan Buddhist tradition, the Venerable Khenchen Palden Sherab Rinpoche and Khenpo Tsewang Dongyal Rinpoche, from whom I learned a good portion of the mental training that allowed me to write about the wonderful wisdom of the Mirror of our minds.

I equally acknowledge the primordial influence that the six volumes of Ser Uno (Being One), www.elseruno.com, channeled by its author/channeler (anonymous), had over this book.

3

Finally, my thanks to my Mother, Doña Berta, for hours spent reading the Christian Bible during my childhood, assuring me that at some point it would strengthen me during the difficult times in my life.

The Master is nothing more than a disciple, who likes to help others find their mastery.

The weapons of the true Warrior of Light are compassion and the patience to wait for the other person to learn what he has already learned.

Don't reply with your Shadows to the Warrior of Shadows, reply with your Light so that he may discover his own.

Iván Figueroa-Otero, MD

THE MELODIOUS SILENCE OF THE COSMOS

Silence yearns to quench the Soul's

unending thirst for Love,

yet in its splendor, it fails to stifle the continuous yet

fleeting chatter of the ego;

for the Soul has long forgotten its majestic tranquility.

How will I be able, then, to arouse the remembrance of

its melodious song again?

I have already realized that this will not occur by

increasing the volume

of the dissonant notes of my mundane life.

Nor by recalling the memories

of my frivolous experiences,

which only ignite more the flames of my insatiable

desire for them,

those infernal passions that muted even more

my sense of hearing.

How can I stifle then the deafening shame

of the condemning voices that punish my heart?

Perhaps only by realizing that all my lapses

were committed with the innocence of intention,

and stipulated by the ignorance of my divine lineage.

Clearly established by our great Teacher, Jesus,

who in his last words said,

"Father, forgive them, for they do not know what they

are doing." (Luke 23:34)

My heart then finally finds peace, as I understand

that in the forgiveness of my transgressions,

and those done to me by others,

resides the final solution to my paradox.

And then, suddenly, a thunderous emptiness permeates

every corner of my Universe,

reawakening in my heart

the Melodious Silence Of The Cosmos.

INTRODUCTION

I congratulate all of those who have reached level 103 of our School of Life, because you were not intimidated by the tests' intensity, nor did you copy from your fellow students in their various learning levels. In level 101, we tried to inspire you to answer the three enigmas of our earthly experience: Who are we? Where do we come from? And where are we heading? By analyzing the testimonials of our individual experience, scientific evidence, and the philosophy outlined by the great sages that preceded us along the way, we are trying to help you answer them individually by looking at the deepest part of your being.

In the first book, we emphasized that every failure always resulted in a learning process, which allows us to restructure our study plan to keep taking the tests until we learned the lesson. We should not think of these tests as punishment from our universal school's regents, but rather as a loving act of patience and trust in our capacity to ace them. Remember that the dropouts were those who gave up and stopped taking their tests.

In level 1.2, we wanted to address younger minds whose daily perspective depends on modern technology, so we transformed the traditional scientific and religious viewpoint into a more cybernetic one. Here we became programmers and domain browsers, varying in personal experiences according to program purity and their degree of corruption. Therefore, we concluded the best way to improve our individual browsing experience is by reprogramming, updating our software, and purging our operating systems from all viral invasions. In each of the previous volumes, we introduced techniques that facilitated the reprogramming and learning process, and we shall go deeper into this as we publish the following levels.

In level 103, we shall discover new angles on the three questions presented in level 101. We shall discuss the techniques that will help us effectively wipe out all viral contamination (guilt), which we have allowed into our learning programs. We could compare these alterations with emotional scars in our mind's mirror, which have not yet healed, suffered while our soul (Warrior of Light) journeyed through the battles throughout the School of Life.

First, when we do a close study on how it was that we received these hurtful lessons, we'll find that they were self-inflicted by the imagined archetypal enemies in our minds. Later, when we identify the causes and origins of these mythical "dragons", we will identify the techniques we need to use to heal them. And, finally, how we can prevent them from recurring.

From the first phase, we have put together a first aid kit for the battlefield, emphasizing that the best medicine in stock is the antidote of forgiveness. The most effective vaccine is the awareness of the shared legacy of love that unites us, from where compassion, and patience to avoid the emotional conflicts that lead to war in the School of Life, are born.

We will study how the relationship between our biological DNA's hereditary programs, the epigenetic details of our lifestyles, and the programming learned in life's different stages could run wild, manifesting as physical and mental diseases. We will again insist on our responsibility for the onset of suffering in our lives, caused by our disconnection from the universe's primordial program, love, and our ignorance of the interdependence that unites us as Warriors of Light.

As we customarily do, after each chapter, we will have study questions and exercises to develop the necessary skills to heal our wounds and prevent future battles. I invite you to boldly join this journey to the most profound and mysterious part of our being and, with plenty of patience and compassion, help heal the emotional wounds of your Inner Warrior of Light.

As I have said before:

The weapons of the true Warrior of Light are compassion and the patience to wait for the other person to learn what he has already learned.

Before accepting you into the Warriors of Light's ranks, you must take the Oath of the Warrior of Light.

The Oath of the Warrior of Light

I am a Warrior of Light, who never abandons his mission nor surrenders before the dark forces. I accept that my mission is to learn to love and let myself be loved and bring hope to others. That everyone is a beloved son of the light, and that without us, love would not manifest, but would be snuffed out in Creation. I know that my worst enemy is the ego, which creates the illusion of tridimensional time, birth, and death. This is the son of deceit, originated by our mind, facing the loneliness of disconnection from the light, our creative source. I understand that emotions and attachment to emotions come from memories of universal feelings, and from having lived in the never-

ending presence of love. The variability and subjectivity of emotional experiences and the suffering from the tonal experience of duality, arise due to the transitory and individual nature of said emotions. I pledge to remember my way back to the light and to help others to remember theirs.

GLOSSARY

1. Antimatter- The opposite of matter, which science postulates existed in equal amounts with the matter after the Big Bang, but which scientists have lost since then. Matter is believed to come from it, but they don't know how. You can see how crystal clear and precise science is! At present, antimatter is nearly undetectable by our instruments' scientific measurements. In this book, it represents the realm of the Warrior of Light.

2. Archetypes- A model or example of ideas or knowledge from which others are derived to shape each individual's thoughts, attitudes, array, society, even each system. For Plato, it was the state of abstract ideas from which everything observable and measurable in our material world was born.

3. Attachment- The perceived need or emotional vice of repeating pleasant experiences, be they physical or mental. In its most immature form, this may be the worst addiction that a human being may experience, and is the principal source of suffering. It can be an appropriate feeling in some cases, and an inappropriate one in others.

4. Battle-originated schizophrenia- State of mental confusion where the self-manifests a dual personality, as Warrior of Light or Warrior of Shadows, which makes him live in an unbalanced universe and causes a lot of confusion and suffering. Most of the people that suffer it believe there are only Warriors of Shadows and consider those that think they are Warriors of Light to be crazy.

5. Chimeric DNA- DNA molecule that occurs naturally, containing sequences from two different species.

6. Dimension- The way we perceive our conscience as existing within the space - three dimensions: width, length, and depth, or height, plus the perception of time. This way of observing the universe is not the same for all animals. For example, ants only see two dimensions and do not perceive height. Maybe that's why they don't fall off walls. The attribute of observing a tridimensional universe depends on our binocular vision and how our brain processes it. When we lose sight in one eye, we lose tridimensional vision, but not that of the other senses. For example, if we don't keep our distance from other objects, we will bump into them and feel it in our body, and the blind can read the tridimensional shapes of Braille with their fingers.

7. DNA- Deoxyribonucleic acid, where all genetic history of the human genome is stored, consists of two parts. 1) The codifier (5% of the genome) is our biological journey within the tridimensional world of time and space as a Warrior of

Shadows, where all genetic action in our chromosomes is stored and coded. 2) The non-codifier or "junk," which archives our multidimensional anti-material trip of the spirit as a Warrior of Light. The latter is stored in the part that science has termed junk DNA because it does not seem to participate in traditional genetic coding.

8. Ego, or realistic mirror- It means the self in Latin. This text refers to the self, which makes us feel as individuals and observers of the universe around us - individualism. It allows us to perceive what is mine and what belongs to others, observe the effects of time (birth, aging, sickness, and death) upon us and interpret the quality of life with the feelings generated by our five senses, in good and bad experiences. Personality is born from it. In this book, it is the realistic mirror that only reflects the artificial light of emotions.

9. Entropy- A measuring pattern. In physics, this applies to the second law of thermodynamics, which states that isolated systems tend towards disorder, that is, things tend towards chaos as time goes by. I compare it to the Yang or centrifugal force of Oriental tradition.

10. Epigenetics- Epigenetics is a branch of biology that tries to explain why living organisms activate some genes and suppress others, thus adjusting their particular physical characteristics and susceptibility to develop certain diseases, which contrasts with the deterministic concept of every genetic predisposition. This suggests that external factors, such as lifestyles, could influence DNA into changing its actions without altering its genetic configuration. Junk DNA may control these changes, and from now on, I will call it "luminous DNA."

11. Forgiveness- The *Windex* (healing balm) to clean all impurities and smudges from our mirror, or transcendental mind.

12. Free will- Part of the attributes of a being who chooses the most beneficial option at a given point in his individual experience within his abilities or limitations. Free will is not the same for everyone: it varies according to personal spiritual development, intelligence, social status, politics, ethics, and health. It's associated with the self's will to act with relative freedom, according to the options available to his experience during his interdimensional journey. This vision, when focused on individualism, generates the extreme individual action known as selfishness.

13. Genome- The set of genes within chromosomes which may be construed as the totality of genetic information for a particular organism or species.

14. Hologram- A tridimensional projection obtained from a flat image, using laser ray techniques. It is used nowadays in shows and movies to broadcast a person's image to distant places. We soon shall be seeing this technology in our homes. The important thing is to understand that a scientist, Dr. Bhom, established that an original object could be replicated entirely from any of its parts. This suggests that each part stores the complete image information and that there is an intrinsic form of communication among all of them, which does not depend on space and time.

15. Horizontal gene transfer- Also known as lateral gene transfer (LGT), the process by which an organism transfers genetic material to another cell that is not a descendant (absent of a reproductive process). On the other hand, vertical transfer occurs when an organism receives genetic material from its ancestors, for example, from its parents or from an ancestor

from which it has evolved. Most genetics studies focus on the prevalence of vertical transfers, but there is currently evidence indicating that horizontal transfer is a significant phenomenon. Artificial horizontal gene transfer is what also happens in genetic engineering.

16. Luminous DNA or "junk" DNA- Non-coding DNA that was thought to have no use, which is very important within the human genome since it makes up a control panel with millions of "switches" that regulate the genetic activity. Without these switches, genes would not work, and mutations could happen that, in turn, would unleash diseases. It is said that epigenetic environmental influence controls the process of activation. That part, which paradoxically occupies 95-97% of DNA, correlates very well with the 95% that our antimatter universe holds. My intuition leads me to speculate that this might be the location of the healing code and all of history, or the Akashic Records, which will open

up the multidimensional doors of the antimatter universe.

17. Masters at Arms: Great Bodhisattvas, White Brotherhood, Prophets, etc. - These are the veteran Warriors of many battles, that have succeeded in defeating their Warriors of Shadows in both inner and external battles. Though they have earned their tickets or coordinates to go back, they return to help in the contest due to their compassion and commitment to the Warriors of Light still fighting.

18. Matryoshkas- A matryoshka, mamushka or Russian nested doll (Russian: Матрёшка /mʌ 'trʲoʂkə/) is a set of traditional Russian dolls created in 1890, original in that they are hollow within, housing a new doll inside, and that doll, in turn, houses another, and another, in variable amounts that may range from five to as many as are wanted, but always in odd numbers, though

due to volumetric limitations, there rarely are more than twenty.

19. Matter- The stuff of which our understandable, measurable, and visible universe is made of, constituting five percent of everything and woven into the nature of time and space, with a beginning and an end. In this book, this is the realm of the Warrior of Shadows.

20. Meditation- A "wireless" communication technique in a format similar to our original universal language, which is one of the tactics taught to us by our masters at arms to re-establish or recall our battle supply lines from our light source, the Magical Mirror.

21. Newton's third law (action-reaction principle)- When a body exerts a force upon another, the latter exerts an equal and opposite force upon the former. In spiritual terms, the law of cause and effect, or dharma-karma, would seem to apply impersonally in a holographic universe

upon our actions, good or bad, while interacting with other beings.

22. Personality- The programming (software) that we believed to define what we are. It's generated from a combination of parents' hereditary characteristics and the acquired or learned experiences of our parents, friends, teachers, religions, books, social environment, and communications media.

23. Primordial mind: the Magical Mirror or time machine- the origin of the two minds, the transcendental or anti-material mind, and the relative or material mind, which are manifestations of awareness, respectively, of the Warrior of Light and the Warrior of Shadows. It represents the potential state of all of the universe's creative process that existed before the Big Bang. It's the vehicle or time machine that allows the Warrior to complete his exploratory voyage.

24. Quantum entanglement- An observable phenomenon regarding the relationship between individual particles that interact in an interdependent quantum state. The reactions of a group of individual particles exhibit a group response as if they were physically and energetically connected and as if there were no physical separation between them. They would seem to be interconnected, differences notwithstanding. The responses of individual particles would seem instantaneous, without a measurable temporal separation.

25. Recombinant DNA- Recombinant DNA, or recombined DNA, is an artificial DNA molecule formed deliberately in vitro by fusing DNA sequences from two different organisms that generally are not found together. This can be done to study gene expression or produce proteins to treat a genetic disease, vaccines, or financial or scientific ends.

24

26. Relative or rational mind - Warrior of Shadows- The state of confusion of the Warrior of Light when harmed by the many emotional wounds from his battles in the school of life. The image is reflected in the Magical Mirror, or primordial mind, whose surface is smudged or foggy.

27. Selfishness- A way to live together in the Warrior of Shadows' universe, based on the independence and individualism that make us feel artificially separated in races, colors, religions, knowledge, and power, where action and its effects are not interdependent. It's a world of mine and yours, but not of ours.

28. Serendipity- Serendipity is a fortuitous and unexpected discovery produced when you are seeking something else. It may also reference a subject's ability to acknowledge that he has made an important discovery, though it is unrelated to his investigation. In more general

terms, it may also be used to mean chance, coincidence or accident.

29. Spiritually lame- The codependent relationship of Warriors of Shadows (selfish persons) who use other beings as crutches to walk on life's path. It's a toxic emotional relationship that binds both aggressor and his victim in an emotional trap from which it's very difficult to escape.

30. Star of Peace- The veteran, resulting from the Warrior of Shadows' reconciliation with the experience obtained in his life's battlefields, with the Warrior of Light and his skills obtained in his inner battle with his Warrior of Shadows, or his ego. At the end of the fight, the Warrior realized that light and shadow can cohabit in the universe, in its infinite degrees of brightness, and that neither could exist without the other. This Warrior learned to live with his feet on the ground but eyes on heaven and realized that,

without his shadow, he could never have discovered his light.

31. Synergy - The opposite force to entropy, comparable to the Yin or centrifugal force that completes the creation's mystic dance.

32. The Akashic records- These are the universal memory of existence. In this multidimensional virtual space, all experiences of the Warrior of Light are filed, including all knowledge and experiences of past lives, the current life, and future potential. It seems to me that these exist within a virtual holographic space woven by the energy of Love. The code to access this space is within the "junk" DNA, which only the savviest Warriors of Light can decipher.

33. The musical harmony of the spheres- It's an old theory. In this multidimensional virtual space of Pythagorean provenance, the idea is that harmonious numerical ratios rule the universe. The movement of celestial bodies – sun, moon,

and stars — is ruled by musical ratios; according to that theory, the distances between planets would correlate with musical intervals.

34. The law of cause and effect (law of Love)- The application of Newton's third law to experiences resulting from Warriors' actions during their interdimensional voyage, causes different emotional outcomes, without an individual punitive purpose, but rather to re-establish balance in the global experience altered by causes. It's very similar to our disciplinary actions with our children when they are growing up, which at times are not very pleasant according to their limited criteria, but that are always motivated by love.

35. Time- A very subjective definition of the observer's experience when he interprets a series of events with his five senses and, based on the memory's cerebral capacity, divides them into present-future imaginary segments. To

establish time, we use references based on the seasons' observable changes or climates and day and night alternation. Based on these changes, humankind has divided time into sections comprised of seconds, minutes, hours, days, months, years, centuries, etc. Now you understand why it's so difficult to keep appointments on time!

36. Transcendent- That which transcends the physical plane, which some people call the metaphysical. It refers to the anti-material universe, where the concepts of time and space do not exist and correspond to the world of quantum physics, the realm of the Warrior of Light.

37. Transcendental mind: Warrior of Light- The highest state that a human being can attain during his battles in the school of life. It's the image reflected in the Magical Mirror or

primordial mind with an clear surface (without smudges).

38. Warrior of Light- Represents the purest human manifestation of light and Love, what in the Christian tradition is the Christ (son of God), and for the Buddhists is the Buddha. It's when the Warrior of Shadows acknowledges his light.

39. Warrior of Shadows- He's a Warrior of Light who, during his many battles and emotional wounds, loses his awareness of his inner light and dedicates himself to living in the shadows of his divine heritage.

CHAPTER I

THE MAGICAL MIRROR REFLECTS ITS CREATION IN AN IMAGINATIVE EXPLOSION OF LOVE

And in the beginning, only darkness existed, but in its dream it saw, within its Magical Mirror or primordial mind, all of the possibilities of its reflecting creation, and an enormous explosion awoke it, and upon opening its eyes it saw its image in the mirror and was no longer alone.

Where does the universe come from? In an initial unconscious state, seemingly bereft of all attributes and characteristics (like the Chinese Tao or Buddhist emptiness), the first dual manifestation of visible light, or Yang, and darkness, or Yin, spontaneously appears. From then on, all potential

31

color hues of the images in the universe shall manifest in infinite combinations, like in a rainbow. It's similar to the spontaneous formation of a matrix, which is infinitely interwoven by hierarchical lineages. As they descend, they become less pure and denser as they come to be further away from their origins.

This multidimensional matrix constitute the web of our self-awareness, which we could scientifically compare to our spiritual DNA heritage. Finally, the universe could be considered a never-ending continuity of infinite cycles of evolution and involution, like day and night, where light and darkness are in a range of hues that shift from extreme light and extreme darkness. The forces that sustain the matrix in its quantum entanglement of love are both the centrifugal nature, or Yang- separates, rejects, sows, and the centripetal one, or Yin- joins, attracts, harvests. See glossary.

After the Big Bang of love, there is an expansion phase. Still, it includes the Yin or centripetal period, which in its supreme manifestation, will end by gathering light in a great black hole from which another universal expansion cycle will be born. The centrifugal force, or Yang, aims to help Warriors of Light to discover the treasures hidden in the shadows of creation, in the reflection of the Magical Mirror.

From this Big Bang moment, the self begins its infinite voyage of discovery in the immensity of its Magical Mirror, or primordial mind, from which the Warrior of Light, or transcendental mind, and the Warrior of Shadows or relative mind are born. They shall face off in the battles of the vast school of life, or the universe. During that mental navigation among the dimensions, the Warrior, as his mirror gets fogged up by his emotional experiences or scars, begins to lose memories of his departure point, his home. He becomes an aimless wanderer, and loneliness leads him to the dark world of emotions. This process makes us feel like wandering travelers, abandoned in time. We will see that experience and its consequences in detail in another chapter.

Wandering Travelers in Time

We must understand that our universal voyage's real purpose is a journey of discovery towards the most remote locations of our self, where the primordial mind or Magical Mirror turns into a time-traveling machine, and where our memory of the tour is the only map that assures us our way back. The interdimensional traveler of light must remember the mission: to convey the navigational coordinates to other wandering travelers, who have become lost in their journey and have forgotten their way back. *The beginning was like a tourist trip without a point of departure, with no pre-programmed stops and without a final destination.*

More than a trip, it resembles an expedition to explore new universes, where the traveler, as if he were in an improvised comedy, chooses his stops or jokes with his free will as he best improvises them and the audience applauds.

We Are All "Mongrels"

The experience of sharing the trip with other travelers differs from the initial purity that we saw reflected in our mirror-mind when we find the different images reflected in other travelers' mirrors. Then, we travelers turn into "mongrels," bearing a progressively changing mental blend of our original "purebred" lineage. *Remember this, since we shall need it for our return trip.* This process is complete when the time traveler arrives at the third dimension, where time, space, matter, the rational mind, contrasting opposites, the human biological organism, and its five senses appear for the first time.

It's within the reflection of this dimension's mirror that the Warrior starts to confront the shadows that will lead him to the battlefield and, for the first time, towards fear and suffering. This is where free will gets complicated, facing all of the tempting options that our mirror reflects when confronting the emotions that influence its decision. In this experience, the law of love, or cause and effect, transforms into the law of karma to help the Warrior correct the mistakes that led him to battle and suffering.

The Smudges in the Mirror: The Origins of the State of War

We could compare the primordial mind that originates the universe as we know it with a Magical Mirror that reflects the image the observer created with his subjective experience during his multidimensional journey. The reflection's purity will be influenced by the glass' transparency and the observer's clarity of vision. Our negative subjective experiences could cloud the mirror with smudges, muddied by our emotions. It would then seem that the mind could create both paradises and infernos in our Magical Mirror, depending on the experiences of our journey on the battlefield.

The first signs of the great battle happened when the Warrior of Light started clouding his mirror-mind's surface with the perception of having a separate existence from his surrounding universe, not being part of it, and he started confusing his shadow with his mirror's actual image. The Warrior's cognitive process in his journey worsened his spiritual nearsightedness. The image in his mirror resembled his shadow, and here he manifests the Warrior of Shadows, his future archenemy.

The attributes the Warrior begins to recognize in his mirror were inherent in the primordial mind. Plato and the Buddha stated: "Knowing is remembering what we already have forgotten." They appeared in its dual manifestation of light and shadows after the Big Bang when the Warrior of Light recognized them.

This holographic symbiosis is the climax of the multidimensional voyage whence both Warriors, love (light), and knowledge (shadows) unite and beget the Star of Peace: comprehension, Christ, Buddha. It's the Warrior of Light within the Warrior of Shadows.

The Primordial Mind, the Transcendental Mind, or Antimatter, and the Relative Mind, or Matter

You should review the antimatter universe's concepts and the material universe in my first books and understand that the anti-material arises from the material. However, science does not know how this happens. The battles between the Warriors of Light and the Warriors of Shadows only take place in the three dimensions of the material universe, and that is the process that we shall be referencing.

What Are the Attributes of the Two Natures: Light and Shadows?

Relative or material mind	Transcendental or anti-material mind
The self as a Warrior of Shadows Perceivable-definite Space-time	The self as a Warrior of Light Imperceptible-relative Without time-space
It's deterministic: It's born and dies in the dimension of space and	It's probabilistic: Nothing is impossible in this state.

time. *It has fear and cowardice.*	Death is a change of manifestation from matter to energy. *It's immensely courageous and makes sacrifices for his brothers in battle.*
It's reductionist: The parts of this universe seem to act independently from others with individualism and selfishness. Every event has an external cause which precedes it. *It always seeks to blame others for its defeats in battle.*	It's holistic: The universe is a unified holographic whole, whose parts instantaneously interact with one another. Every event in its components impacts all other parts interdependently. *It shares the responsibility of everything that happens on the battlefield, does not believe in guilt.*

The observer sees the universe as something outside himself and does not feel a part of it. The reality is external and independent of the observer. *During the battle, he only cares about his life.*	The observer is an interdependent part of his universe, he is a microcosm of his macrocosm, and maintains a holographic relationship with the whole. The universe surrounding him can be changed with his thought intent. *He never leaves his companions' flanks unprotected, and never abandons the wounded or dead in battle.*
It's based on the knowledge of "absolute truths or laws". Time is absolute	It's based on the knowledge of a universe that changes continually in infinite cycles with "tendencies to exist" or

everywhere in the universe. The universe is tridimensional. *He does not know when to accept defeat and seek peace.*	"tendencies to happen". Time does not exist. The universe is multidimensional. *He can recognize defeat as an experience to start over and forgive without avenging.*

The more destinations he travels to on his mind/time machine and the longer the Warrior of Light's journey becomes, more memories of our origins are clouded, as does its initial purpose. Free will is born from experiences in the traveled paths.

Free Will Would Seem to Be Like a Frequent Flyer Coupon with Unlimited Mileage

This coupon allows us to change our bearing indiscriminately, with the only inconvenience being that it does not include living expenses. This means that we will have to work or learn at each destination to find enjoyment before we leave for the next destination.

Each new dimensional destination you arrive at on your time machine represents a horizon of new, contrasting knowledge that activates choosing the new bearing, enabling free will as a learning tool. Some of these paths turn out to be more agreeable, pleasant, or faster than others, and the Warrior labels them on his map for future reference.

We must recall that each new path and the creation of emotional experiences lead him further away from the light, and fogs up his mind's mirror even more. This makes his shadow seem more prominent in the mirror's reflection. The ratio of the manifestation of the Warrior of Shadows' characteristics increases as the Warrior of Light's decreases through his progression in his downward dimensional voyage.

One day, drawn like Ulysses by his sirens' song, the Warrior discovers the realm of shadows or the

42

battlefield of suffering and pleasure, which is the material universe of space-time where he will meet his archenemy, the Warrior of Shadows. Here our Warrior begins an unending series of battles where he receives and inflicts endless wounds.

The Ego: The Witch from the Hansel and Gretel Fairy Tale

The problem is that, same as with Ulysses in his journey, the emotion's tempting song is similar to that of the fable's sirens. It is the main reason for creating the ego and his firstborn, selfishness, with all of its accompanying features (see the definition for both). It implies that, as we delve into the worlds of tridimensional time, the coordinates of places visited and those of our origins are erased even more.

This is what happened in the Hansel and Gretel fairy tale, when the birds ate the breadcrumbs' map because the witch charms the birds to obstruct the way back to our home, tempting us with the candy house of the material world to trap us in the light's shadows.

43

This is how the Warrior of Light starts sinking into the shadows, as the light's reflection in his Magical Mirror clouds up. This will advance when all he will see in his mind's mirror are Warriors or Shadows, even in his image. At that moment, the Warrior has forgotten his luminous origins and the purpose of his voyage.

As within so without. The mirror of our mind creates our worst enemy from our negative emotions, and that is us! The Warrior of Shadows and the emotions that imprison him in this universe help him erase all memories of the coordinates he saved in his time machine to return to his origins.

The Origin of Emotions

Emotions emerge from the Warrior of Light's subjective interpretation of contrasting experiences during the journeys in his time machine. These, based on his previous experiences, may be classified as good, bad, or neutral. The observer tends to repeat the good ones, avoid the bad ones, and ignore the neutral ones. Repeating or keeping good experiences generates happiness, and not obtaining or losing the good ones causes suffering.

The desire to always keep experiencing good emotions is known as an attachment (see glossary), and this attachment to the better emotions generates suffering when we don't get them.

The Warrior of Shadows Will Never Be Happy

Our tridimensional universe is the Warrior of Shadows' realm, where the laws of time and space apply. In this universe, thermodynamics' laws place the process of matter into a continuous flux of matter to energy, and every physical structure separates into its components due to its entropy (see glossary). That's when we see deterioration, aging, and oxidation. This creates insecurity or fear in the observer due to the changing or cyclic nature of the universe, augmented by a lack of control in avoiding these changes.

This insecurity and the attachment to good experiences generate suffering in the Warriors inhabiting this realm. If we amplify the experience with every observer's subjectivity as to what is good or bad, we will realize why the Warriors in this area disagree so much.

The Origin of the Suffering of the Warrior of Shadows

The Warrior who does not understand where he comes from and who he is feels lost in a constant battle with time and change that he created with his habits. He also suffers a disagreement with other beings regarding what happiness is.

Living, if we go about it with selfishness and lack of awareness of our interdependence with the universal laws and other people, turns into a nightmare of suffering, with brief moments of happiness.

We can finish the chapter understanding that the origin of the Warrior's battles is selfishness and competition for power, to obtain that which grants us pleasure and the capacity to preserve it.

Homework

Exercises to find the universe's invisible matrix that reflects our mind-mirror.

1. Let's observe everything that surrounds us with our five senses, like the image in a mirror.

   a) Can we see, smell, feel, hear, and taste everything that we know exists? We are aware we can't. Let's think about the things we know exist but can't perceive.

   b) Have we ever seen the wind that moves the tree's branches?

   c) Has anyone seen or felt X-rays when they're taken or seen or felt the sun's rays' infinite emissions, which bombard us and pierce our bodies?

   d) Have we ever seen the constant thoughts that our minds generate?

e) Can anyone tell us precisely where the mind is and describe its configuration?

f) Can anyone see and locate where our emotions happen?

g) Do we see all of the millions of microscopic and submicroscopic organisms that live throughout our bodies' surface? Gazing at the body from the outside, we can't see all the types of cells that constitute our organs. No one doubts most of these things, but no one has ever seen them without special instruments.

2. These simple observations make us realize that not everything that exists is perceivable and that perceivable things are not the only ones that exist. Are you already finding where the rest of the universe is?

3. Observe your image in the mirror and note all you see without judging and seeking its origin.

Visualize everything you think, see, smell, touch, savor or hear as reflections of your mirror-mind. Observe how your image changes as you recall disagreeable and pleasant events in your past. Try to see or hear the electrical currents that the nerve conduction of those thoughts creates. Feel the surface of your body and that of objects surrounding you. Observe their texture, solidity, and elasticity. See your hands and understand that they are made of muscular tissue, cartilage, and bone, which is composed of invisible cells, molecules, and organic compounds. Finally, they are made out of invisible subatomic particles.

4. All the other parts of your body are made up of the same elementary particles - atoms. But why do we see them so differently? How did we learn to differentiate our universe? Are the names granted to these attributes the same in every language? Observe how, during your lives, your actions have influenced other persons, and other persons' have influenced your own.

5. Finally, meditate in silence about what you have observed and answer these questions: Where's my visible me or individuality? Where's my invisible part? Where is what suffers and loves? Observe if there are changes in your image in the mirror. If you find it, send me an e-mail and tell me where you found it!

Bonus Questions

1. Why is it suggested in this chapter that learning is only remembering what we have forgotten?

2. What would seem to be the purpose of the Warrior of Light's voyage?

3. What is the reason, if any, for experiencing suffering?

4. Why can't light and shadow live without one another?

5. How can we recognize the enemy in our battlefield?

CHAPTER II

THE BATTLE BETWEEN THE WARRIORS OF LIGHT AND SHADOWS: THE BEGINNING

The law of cause and effect exists in the dimensional planes that continually connect with the primordial mind (Magical Mirror, light, and love). However, the free will concept that rules the dual and contrasting manifestations occurring in our tridimensional space-time universe does not exist in those higher planes.

The Smudges that Cloud Our Mirrors: The Causes of Our Confusion and Disconnection from Our Origins

In the previous chapter, we said that the reflection's purity would be affected by the transparency of the mirror's glass and the clarity of vision of the observer. We also implied that these smudges were made by our five senses, like fingers muddied by the toxic emotions that we experience in our battles in the earthly life. It's as if our minds' mirror reflected every emotional scar from the battlefield, like a crack on the surface. The more battles there are, the more scars and less purity in the mirror's reflection.

As in the tridimensional plane, where time and space rule, there are "languages" or codes in the antimatter universe's multidimensional planes to promote communications between its inhabitants. We must understand that only one type of communication or common language existed in the higher realms, which allowed their inhabitants to communicate among themselves and their source of light, the Magical Mirror, without interference. This connection is later lost during the Warriors' journey in the tridimensional material universe.

That would explain the real biblical meaning of the tower of Babel, where the Warriors of Shadows did not want to continue their journey. They only sought to ascend and recover the codes of the Warriors of Light's common language without earning a return trip ticket, which they could only obtain through their learning experiences in the voyage itself.

In the Beginning, the Yang or Centrifugal Manifestation Controls the Process

The initial tour in our time machine or mirror-mind had, as in any journey, a departure schedule divided into stops that represented the Yang or centrifugal-explosive phase of the Big Bang. The initial disadvantage of having a universal language was that it favored the centripetal inertia of the Big Bang's Yin phase. This manifested in the Warrior's conformist attitude about staying in his first destination. It did not awaken the exploratory appetite for discovering new dimensional destinations and experiences, which is encouraged by the creative process' centrifugal phase.

The Dark Side of Disconnection Was the Progressive Loss of Memory or Access to their Akashic Records

The linguistic disruption represented in the tower of Babel's allegory initially tipped the scale towards the exploratory and expansive phase of the interdimensional voyage. The longer the interdimensional stops or layovers lasted, the more the Warriors forgot their universal language. This fostered a steady increase in dialects that hindered and obstructed sharing voyaging experiences and distorted their recall of the way back to their origins.

The most severe disconnection took place at the space-time dimension, where we forgot we were voyagers in time with a clear mission. As I mentioned in previous chapters, the existential loneliness of this experience brought the birth of the ego, emotions, and suffering that we previously discussed.

This inability to share a common language, plus geographical, racial, social, and hereditary influences, originated a wide variety of subjective experiences that fanned the fire that began all the Warriors of Light's historical battles.

This is the light's and shadows' mental continuum start to separate, representing the anti-material DNA lineage and the material-biological DNA lineage. We then see that our anti-material DNA includes the navigational code to return to our home with our time machine.

The Warrior's primary purpose is to recall or decipher that code by healing all the cloudiness in his mirror, created by the emotional experiences in his battles. The disconnection between these two lineages is the main reason for our ego, representing the fictitious light that the Warrior of Shadows creates to guide him on his journey.

This ego turns into a distorted mirror that only reflects selfish images, selectively pleasing some of us and hurting others. Selfishness and its close cousin, ambition, later become the driving force that rules the lives of the Warriors of Shadows, who choose to start wars against all who do not share their false vision.

The Quest for Happiness and the Avoidance of Suffering: The Root Causes for the Battle of the Warriors

The search for happiness is one of the few actions in which human beings agree absolutely, though we may not agree on what it is and how to find it. We must understand that even though the Warrior progressively forgot his origins and luminous lineage, he still conserves memories of his higher state. Those memories generate a feeling of emptiness or loneliness, subconsciously, that manifests as melancholy and sadness, like how we feel when losing a loved one. This is the feeling that the Warrior tries to fill with the emotional, fictitious, and changing emotions that the ego generates within the material universe.

These changing emotions that always lead to the cycle of birth, aging, and death are called Samsara in the Oriental tradition, the period of rebirth and death.

Both loneliness and separation are ego illusions, which cannot acknowledge the vast fullness of the light and love that permeates all the space in creation.

Communications among Warriors are complicated, since the Warrior of Light enters into his shadows very gradually, as his mirror's toxic emotional experiences keep clouding his vision. Furthermore, they increase with his efforts to share his tainted experience with others, which contaminates other Warriors' mirrors. This might explain the unconscious mistakes that we have historically committed when transmitting the Magical Mirror's message in a sectarian and religious form.

The Rules of Engagement and the War Fronts in This Battlefield Are Not Very Clear

Though both sides seek victory, they don't have the same goals, and thus the rules of engagement vary depending on the Warrior and his situation. The difficulty in establishing the rules of engagement is further complicated since the war happens between

Warriors of Shadows in different emotional confusion levels. However, their external uniform is very similar. In this conflict, the Warriors of Light may only participate in an "advisory" capacity to the Warriors of Shadows.

In this conflict, the Warriors of Light can only participate as counselors to those Warriors of Shadows who allow it.

The Warrior of Light's Purpose in Battle- To free the light within the Warrior of Shadows, activating his healing forgiveness code and helping him heal his emotional wounds to eliminate all the impurities from his mirror that do not let him see its light. This Warrior does not believe in the force of confrontation but rather in logic, comprehension, commitment, and forgiveness, and has infinite patience to achieve it.

The Warrior of Shadows' Purpose in Battle- To instill terror and fear in the ranks of opposing Warriors with massive frontal tactics and bacteriological, surprise, sabotage and infiltration attacks, and to

58

increase the emotional wounds that cloud their mirrors even more, which stop them from recalling their origins. The ego also tempts them, offering economic, political, and religious power to defend the banner of shadows.

The Two Battlefronts of the Warrior of Light

As he faces the emotional battles in his life, the Warrior of Light realizes that he created an imaginary war with two battlefronts. The inner battle with his Warrior of Shadows, and the external conflict with other Warriors of Shadows. To ensure victory in his fight, he has to accept his responsibility in creating his imaginary dragons based on his ignorance of that stage in his journey. This war's irony is that you can never win by killing your imaginary enemies, since they create reinforcements of fictitious Warriors through the self-inflicted injuries in our inner battles.

This duality in conflict makes it impossible for the Warrior to enjoy lasting moments of peace, since even though you may be victorious in one front you have to keep fighting on the other. The worst battle is the internal one because its imaginary enemies in the subconscious use guerrilla and sabotage techniques, which may not be apparent until the crisis gels.

The Inner Battle with His Warrior of Shadows

The most dangerous Warrior in battle is our inner Warrior, since he works sabotaging and camouflaging his presence in the deepest parts of the mind-mirror. The warning signs are very subtle, like mental diseases (depression, anxiety, bipolar disorder) and physical diseases (cancer, degenerative, autoimmune) and where therapeutic remedies can worsen the condition. It behooves us to heal them, as we caused these emotional injuries.

The External Battle with the Warriors of Shadows, who Accompany You on Your Trip

In this battle, it's easier to recognize our enemies and their tactics because they are Warriors lost in their mirror's shadows and cannot see the light in others, since they cannot see it within themselves.

They like to compete for everything that the shadows give them: pleasure, recognition, and power over other Warriors. Their most significant effort goes towards clouding the light in our mirrors, denigrating our self-esteem and our connection with the light of our Magical Mirrors. We will carry out this battle in our country, home, families, schools, workplaces, and churches. And the Warrior's greatest weapon for survival is patience and compassion for our brothers in the journey, as the great master Jesus said, "Father, forgive them, for they do not know what they are doing." (Luke 23:34)

To be successful, the Warrior must focus his forces on his internal battlefront, since that is what decides the outcome. He obtains the tactics and weapons he will need to win the battle in his external front from his inner victories. In his victory in the internal front, the Warrior of Shadows has already recalled a good portion of his lineage or healing code and transforms again into the Warrior of Light.

61

To reiterate this, I share this phrase.

"The weapons of the true Warrior of Light are compassion and the patience to wait for the other person to learn what he has already learned."

Homework

Let's review our life's history. Remember its happiest moments. Were those moments brought by material accomplishments like honors, diplomas, properties, cars, or riches? Or were they events that are not so practical, like weddings, the birth of a child or grandchild, graduations, or a loved one's success? How many happy events from achieving material goals later had consequences that weren't so nice? Like, for example, the responsibility of having to pay for a new car or a home mortgage. Educational goals and diplomas, did they bring what you expected from them, or did they only add responsibilities and obligations to your life?

All of your planning and goods acquisitions and public acknowledgment, could it forestall the many sad moments in your life, like the death and sickness of a loved one or your parents' divorce within their apparent wealth? How many plastic surgeries will we need to preserve the illusion of eternal youth? No surgery can erase our hearts' (mirrors) emotional scars when they have aged to a point where they can no longer love life's simple things.

Let's review how we owe all our accomplishments to the many battles with the Warriors of Shadows, and let's be thankful. It's an unending list, starting with our parents and ancestors, who also had their shadows. Now let's meditate silently about all our battle experiences and their consequences or defeats. Let's understand how our actions affect others, directly or indirectly, and how their actions have the same effect on us. Do we feel like clear images in the Magical Mirror, or like fictitious reflections of a mirror fogged up by our battles' emotional scars? Let us finish with a silent meditation. Search again for your Warrior of Light.

Bonus Questions

1. If happiness is a state of wellness created by the reflection of the mind-mirror, what should I do when facing experiences of suffering, to lessen them?

2. Does darkness or evil exist within the Warriors? If it does not, why do we carry out actions that create shadows (suffering) in others?

3. Where can we find love in this troubled world? (Suggestion: look for it in an immaculate mirror!)

CHAPTER III

THE WARRIORS' DRUMS: PREPARING FOR BATTLE

Co-programming and Co-responsibility in Maintaining Our Primordial Software

The First Signs of the Unavoidable Conflict

Every situation that generates discord and suffering for the Warriors, both the inner Warrior as well as the external ones, as they increase in intensity and frequency, they signal us that the battle is approaching. Though the concordance in different armies and alliances of these Warriors can be based on racial, religious, economic, or political divisions, the primary motivation that leads a group to attack another is the desire to usurp political, geographical, and economic power, and imposing that which favors the winner. And though it may seem that the war benefits all Warriors of the Shadows, only a minority controls combat decisions and enjoys the benefits.

65

We must heed our bodies' warnings since it first whispers symptoms, then speaks to us with diseases, and finally, if we ignore it, shouts at us with cancer and advanced diseases!

Signals in the Inner Warrior that Foreshadow the Conflict

1. Progressive deterioration of the Warriors' physical health and general welfare, created by toxic lifestyles, promoted by the industries that profit from this situation like the pharmaceutical, medical, and food. This leads to a dramatic increase in degenerative and congenital diseases in children and adults, cancer, and new diseases never previously seen. The toxic effects of all of these insults and our DNA manipulation could cause nefarious epigenetic (see glossary) changes in our next generations.

2. Progressive deterioration in mental-emotional health resulting from the above mentioned physical deterioration, and the chronic stress

state that frustration and anguish generate due to not having and lacking the capacity to obtain the requirements that the ego demands of them to feel happy and fruitful. This difficult situation appears due to social, racial, and economic disadvantages that hinder the Warrior from obtaining the essential requirements for his happiness, or what the media demands. The worst part is that even those who obtain the most achievements never attain happiness or achieve their welfare since the gains do not fill their spiritual emptiness. The mighty ones that control power use this to promote war, arguing that the Warriors' suffering is due to the enemy.

3. This incapacitating feeling leads many Warriors to crime, both blue and white-collar, and to the endless types of hallucinogenic and addictive drugs that destroy their mind-mirrors and make them fall deeper into their shadows and commit the distressing act of suicide.

4. Religious conflicts turn into political and economic weapons for some governments to dominate others, where a new combat weapon arises that is tough to counteract by conventional means: terrorism.

5. An educational imbalance occurs. Education, one of the few ways to avoid oppression and social injustice, is mainly aimed at the powers that control its curriculum and have the financial means to get it.

6. Freedom of the press begins to erode. When news media turn into multinational conglomerates, the powers that rule them impose their editorial features.

7. Health becomes a business. This happens mainly in the U.S., where the capitalist philosophy supported by the constitution does not acknowledge health as a human right.

8. The matricide of our Mother Earth. Human beings have not yet attained global awareness and accepted their responsibility for the health of our shared home, the Earth. The attitude of alienation and misuse of its resources will provoke climate changes that will affect all human beings' quality of life. Some other alienated and evil actions are:

a) Water pollution.

b) Forest destruction.

c) Many species' extinctions.

d) Abuse and consumption of domestic animals.

e) The exploitation of its natural resources.

f) Genetic alteration of plants and fruits.

Preparing for Battle

Having already recognized the signs of war, we must now prepare, individually and collectively, to face it. When preparing, we should not forget that the war in which we should be victorious first is the one waged in our internal battlefield, which, as I previously mentioned, is the one providing weapons and tactics to win the external one. The first thing the Warrior must do is gain awareness of which side he is on and what is his primary goal in the conflict. This is why he must take this oath at the start.

The Oath of the Warrior of Light (repetition)

I am a Warrior of Light, who never abandons his mission nor surrenders before the dark forces. I accept that my mission is to learn to love and to let myself be loved and to bring a message of hope to others. That everyone is a beloved son of the light, and that without us, Love would not manifest, but would be snuffed out in Creation. I know that my worst enemy is the ego, which creates the illusion of tridimensional time, birth, and death. This is the son of deceit, originated by our mind, facing the loneliness of disconnection from the light, our creative source. I understand emotions and attachment to emotions are born from memories of universal feelings, and from having lived in the never-ending presence of Love. The variability and subjectivity of emotional experience, as well as the suffering from the tonal experience of duality, arise due to the transitory and individual nature of said emotions. I pledge to remember my way back to the light and to help others to remember theirs.

The Way Back Is only a Process of Recalling or Deciphering the Secret Code of Our Luminous DNA

Plato explained this in his saying: "All learning is remembering," since he, same as the Buddha, held that all of the universe's creative process was engraved since the beginning in universal archetypes.

The previous oath could unleash a series of mental reactions in the Warriors that could awaken the desire to begin making their way back and remember their mental healing code for their trip in their Magical Mirror or time machine. It will motivate them to reconnect with their mirror's light, and allow their inner Warrior of Light to support them in their armed conflict. Due to cloudiness in the reflection in his mirror-mind, he might confuse the Warrior of Shadows' attributes with those of the Warrior of Light. Like the Big Bad Wolf, the ego masquerades as Little Red Riding Hood to impede his return. To acknowledge that the ego has taken control of the Warrior of Shadows, we must identify his attributes.

Attributes of the Warrior of Shadows Activated By the Ego (According to the Texts in El Ser Uno)

1. They feel that no one understands them.

2. They perceive that others see them as different.

3. They want everyone to think like them.

4. They talk all day long about the same topic.

5. They feel that others are ignorant.

6. They resent that their partner does not desire the same things they do

7. They want their partner or children to march in lockstep with them.

8. They recommend many books to all of their friends.

9. They don't feel they "belong" when they go to a meeting.

10. They begin to withdraw.

11. They throw up walls around them.

12. They look down their noses at other people, disdainfully.

13. Nothing can happen to them because "God" protects them.

14. They feel "chosen and enlightened."

15. They think a given "belief" is the absolute truth.

16. They look at other people with pity.

17. They believe with absolute certainty that they are on the right path and that others are not.

When faced by inklings of our light, that initial reaction, fostered by the ego, will fade if we boldly follow our inner quest. We will then remember the true features of the Warrior of Light, which were clouded by the emotional scars or smudges in our battles' mirror.

The True Attributes of the Warrior of Light (El Ser Uno)

1. It becomes easier for them to communicate with Love and understanding with all types of Warriors.

2. They do not flaunt the power of their light but save if for an appropriate moment. They do not flaunt their attributes since this could alert the enemy.

3. They respect the opinions of everyone around them. After all, they could be wrong.

4. They calibrate their behavior and speech to the group they are partaking with, as long as no one is gossiping about others.

5. They recall that everyone is on the way back with differing degrees of learning.

6. They respect their partners' space and vision.

7. They understand that the learning rate in different people varies.

8. They recommend a book only when asked or when it's needed.

9. They take part in life with Love and happiness.

10. They always know how to have fun when attending a meeting.

11. They do not walk away from the beings that love them because they have not yet seen their

light. Everyone is essential in their learning. They recall that someone was patient with them when they were in similar stages.

12. They open their hearts so that everyone around them may come near them.

13. No one is better than the other, like the three Musketeers: all for one and one for all!

14. There's only one God (a Magical Mirror), with many human versions of the same, as per our mirrors-minds' cloudiness.

15. No one "chose" them; they only awoke and recalled their path and origins.

16. No one has the absolute truth, only our creator.

17. They know that, as they pity others, others shall pity them. Pity denigrates others, while compassion strengthens them.

18. They'll know they are on the right path when they get to know the loving intention of their actions' cause and effect.

How Can We Develop Positive Attributes?

1. We must change our lifestyles to reduce the previous adverse effects and stop acting to abuse Mother Earth; it's fruits, resources, and ourselves.

2. Ensure that everything to absorb through the senses is neither toxic nor processed: what we hear, read, drink, and eat. This can affect our DNA due to its epigenetic influence (see glossary) and make it harder to recall our return coordinates. We must particularly avoid consuming animal products, whether or not they are mistreated.

3. Ally yourself with Warriors that can help you find your inner light, without sectarian prejudices nor states of co-dependence that turn them into

crutches of the spiritually lame (see the glossary and my first book).

4. Scrutinize your image in the mirror deeply and courageously, and heal all of the emotional scars you carry hidden in the shadows of your reflection by confronting them with Love, compassion, and forgiveness.

Homework

Before taking a few minutes to meditate, let's read the Warrior's Oath aloud once again.

Afterward, let's watch our bodies to detect the signs that our conflict has already reached its peak. Let's try to see if these signals came from the external or internal battlefronts. Practice these exercises.

Shamata Meditation Exercise

To decrease the predominance of our Warrior of Shadows, we must learn to soothe it. Quieting the mind is the object of the meditation termed Shamata,

78

where we focus the mind's action in a single direction. Though techniques vary greatly, the most used ones concentrate on sacred objects, a light like a candle's, saying the rosary, or singing a mantra. In the Tibetan Buddhist tradition, focusing thought on the breathing cycle is encouraged, observing how air enters and exits the nose. At the same time, we allow the cycle to proceed naturally. Practice counting breathing cycles that consist of one inhalation and one exhalation, up to seven times. The moment the mind detours thought towards something else, you must restart counting the seven breaths cycle. You will be surprised how fast the mind detours before the seventh cycle! Again, seek where the self or the mind is found within your bodies.

Mindfulness Meditation

In this exercise, let's dedicate our day to a close observation of our interaction with our environment. Let's observe our daily routines, like our personal hygiene and dressing. Which shoe do you put on first? Which sleeve do you put your arm down first? Note your breakfast routine. Observe your breathing cycle, and note the difference in rhythm and temperature between breathing in and breathing out.

During your ritual, observe what your mind is doing. Try to chew your food at least twenty times and be aware of the flavors. Avoid controversial topics and discussions during your meals. Is your mind wandering elsewhere or in other actions? Practice bringing it to the present action. Observe well your interaction with colleagues at work and try to pinpoint how they feel: are they happy or sad? Note how you feel emotionally regarding each one of them. Why do you like (sympathize with) some of them more than others? What factors led you to come to this conclusion?

The next time you feel bothered by a colleague's action or comment, ask yourself if he or she intended to bother you or if you misinterpreted the action. If we undergo a difficult experience of this sort, after calming down, let him or her know that you felt hurt by that action, without blaming or criticizing it. Observe his or her reaction. When you leave home, smile even at your shadow and see the effect that has on others. Before losing emotional control, count until you tire or add complex numbers in your mind. This activates the rational part of your brain and will help you avoid many hard times. Reread all previous chapters and learn to see the universe through the reflection of the Magical Mirror.

Bonus Questions

1. How can I recognize my shadows?

2. What do I observe in my body and emotional state when they appear?

3. Keep a diary of your observations.

4. Read the Warrior's Oath aloud and meditate upon its meaning and commitment.

5. What warning signals of the armed conflict do you already have?

6. Check to see the ratio of good and bad

attributes you still have.

7. Which battle predominates in you, the external or the internal one?

CHAPTER IV

THE INITIAL BATTLEFRONT IS IMAGINARY AND INTERNAL: THE SHADOW'S MYTHICAL DRAGONS

The Warrior's Battles Are Unconventional Since They Lack Fixed Battlefronts.

Since his battles coincide in two theaters, the Warrior has to guard all of his flanks. He will defend the flank of his internal battle wherever he goes, and he'll do the same for his outer flanks at home, at work, in schools, churches, where the other Warriors will focus their attacks.

We already mentioned that the most crucial battle occurs within his headquarters, representing the imaginary contest between the Warrior of Light with the shadow of his imaginary Warrior, created by the distorted images in his mind-mirror by the emotional wounds created by the conflict. We can compare this battle to a state of schizophrenia, caused by the armed conflict called battle-originated schizophrenia (see glossary). Here the Warrior, in the war's post-traumatic condition, lives in a perpetual hallucinogenic state where his enemies seem to be every one that shares his life. This contest will decide the Warrior's capacity to succeed in his external battles, providing him with tactics or techniques that will lead him to success in his outer battlefront.

The Development of the Warrior's Internal Battle: His Shadow Always Follows the Warrior of Light. Without His Shadow, the Warrior Will Not Be Able to Recognize His Light

This phrase hides the secret that guides the Warrior on his way back since it implies that the Star of Peace (see glossary) will only arise from the victory and armistice between the two Warriors. This traveler completed all the stops on his journey and accumulated all the data learned from each tourist experience. He returns to his point of departure, the Magical Mirror, with a wealth of knowledge engraved with Love, understanding, and compassion to nurture the next creative cycle or Big Bang. His way back is driven by the universal process' Yin phase.

All Paths Lead to Heaven, as All Battles Lead to Victory, But Not At the Same Time

To understand the meaning of this phrase, we must remember that even though the Warriors of Light started with a common purpose, they did so at different cycles of their schedules and training, leading them to complete their assignments in various stages in their experience. That's why each one's battles are individual, though, on occasions, they may coincide in the external battlefront. And this learning method is very similar to the one described in my first book about the school of life.

Our Universe as a Classroom. The School of Life

That's why if you examine my first book, "Spirituality 101: for the Dropouts of the School of Life", you will recall that I compare the universal experience to a classroom, where we all are at different levels of spiritual development, and where tests are aimed very specifically at our learning capacity. The most advanced students help those in lower grades, sharing their experience to pass their exams.

As in every armed conflict, the Warrior of Light is reluctant or afraid to confront his enemy in the internal battle. The biggest problem is that the Warrior of Light does not accept that he has an imaginary enemy and has been in an undeclared cold war for some time, which is already affecting his battlefront and his capacity to counterattack. Remember the phrase, "People don't die in a forewarned war." To understand why the Warrior does not recognize his enemy, we must recall that the emotional scars created unconsciously in the external battles distorted the image in his mind's mirror. He confuses his shadow's reflection with his real, initial pristine image.

86

The Shadow of Our Inner Warrior Is Projected Fictitiously in the Mirrors of the Warriors Who Share His Journey, Thus Duplicating the Enemy's Troops

These reflections in his mirror help him remember the bright image that he initially brought, and lead him to recognize his shadow as the cause of all mayhem in his battlefield. The next step in order for the battle plan to take him to victory is to acknowledge his responsibility for the cloudiness in his mirror, created by the emotional scars from his external battles with other Warriors during his journey. He must understand that the menacing shadow of his inner Warrior was fictitiously reflected in the mirrors of the other Warriors in his earthly experience, like dragons in their external battle, duplicating the enemy's forces, which he faced outside his home, schools, and workplaces.

The emotional reactions that create the experience of suffering are created by the lack of appropriate weapons like self-esteem, capability, experience, patience, understanding, and maturity to deal with our ego's attack without suffering emotional wounds. When we review the strategy we used in that encounter, we must realize that we used the "best" one we had available at the time, and not blame ourselves for that action. We must see that these practices are, as the following phrase suggests, only detours to complete the remaining destinations, which we need to fulfill our universal experience.

In our multidimensional voyage, there are no wrong paths.

The Warrior's Shadow Projects Even More as the Amount of His Emotional Wounds Increases

The projection of the Warrior's shadow grows according to the emotional wounds' progress from the external battle, as does his mirror's opacity. That increase in his shadow allows him to darken other Warriors' mirrors with fear, increasing the enemy's army's reinforcements. The opposite happens when the Warrior learns to heal and prevent battle wounds, cleaning stains from his mirror's surface. Then his light starts dispelling shadows and illuminates others, guiding them in the internal and external battles. This situation is very similar to the purification by sacrificial blood and suffering in the Judea-Christian tradition. That's why the phrase, "Wherever a compassionate man walks on turns into Holy Land," where any battle can transform itself into a celebration of peace.

Emotions, Selfishness, Attachment, and Ambition: The Weapons of the Warrior of Shadows, or the Ego

To take full advantage of this discussion, I recommend reviewing Chapter I and the characteristics that differentiated both Warriors. These characteristics determine how they face their battles and the weapons they use in them.

As he was at the beginning of his voyage, the Warrior of Light had all of the characteristics that light conferred upon him at the start and began to cloud up when emotional experiences clouded his vision during the journey machine of his mind-mirror. Check the Warrior Characteristics table in Chapter I again.

The Warrior of Light lives in a holographic world (see glossary) where Love and the empathy born of feeling partly interdependent of every other manifestation of the creation makes him think of the experience of his voyage as "ours" and not as "mine". Light and Love are his lineage or family, which keep him connected in an unwavering matrix that always accompanies him in his exploratory voyage. He can disconnect himself due to interference in his mirror's reflection, created by his emotions.

We must understand there are as many types of Warrior as there are degrees of disconnection. Therefore, there are many levels of darkening or shadows of his light. Thus, the more darkness there is, the more fictitious Warriors or dragons menace us on our voyage. To be successful in his battle, the Warrior of Light must recall and use his light's natural weapons.

Causes of Disconnection from Our Source of Light

The linguistic disconnection represented in the tower of Babel allegory was what initially tipped the scale towards the exploratory and expansive phase of the interdimensional trip. In this stage, the longer the interdimensional stops lasted, the more the Warriors forgot of their universal language. This fostered an unceasing increase in dialects that hindered and obstructed the sharing of voyage experiences and promoted their memory's distortion. The most severe disconnection took place upon arrival at the space-time dimension and the total alienation that we were voyagers in time with a clear mission. As I mentioned in previous chapters, the existential loneliness of this experience gives rise to the birth of the ego, emotions, and suffering.

The universal common language that allowed all Warriors of Light to communicate is lost when the Warrior arrives at the space-time-matter dimension. In that dimension, the rise of emotions, attachments, ego, and selfishness makes it necessary to create new languages based on the five senses and individual racial, geographical, and social characteristics.

These languages divide our original holographic experience into an individual one of mine and not ours. Warriors not recalling their origins, believing that they live in a time without transcendence and that their lives were a process limited to being born and dying, urges them to take advantage of time to try to enjoy pleasant emotions and shun unpleasant ones. Attachment (see glossary) arises from the need to repeat pleasant feelings, and ambition stems from seeking to control and value everything that produces pleasant emotions.

We discussed this process of ensuring pleasure and seeking happiness in Chapter I, and summarize it in this quote:

The search for happiness is one of the few actions in which human beings agree absolutely, though we may not agree on what it is and how to find it.

92

In other chapters, we will discuss how the quest to find our universal language shall be one of our goals to try to remember the return coordinates to our point of departure (Magical Mirror).

The Weapons of the Warrior of Light

The weapons of the true Warrior of Light are compassion and the patience to wait for the other person to learn what he has already learned.

The Warrior of Light's weapons were included in his travel backpack, along with his travel schedule, as a tourist guide entitled The Warrior of Light's Battle Manual. These weapons are the spiritual, ethical values that guide the light's creative-expansive-centrifugal (Yang) process and its gathering-centripetal one, aimed at everybody's welfare. This manual contains the light's codified formats, or weaponry, which help the Warrior face all the new experiences in its journey. These values manifest in specific forms that adapt to facilitate the learning experience at each dimensional awareness level. Let's see the manual's contents.

The Warrior of Light's Battle Manual

This manual is written in the codes or symbols of our original universal language. The keys to decipher each part are found in our mirror-mind with every victory we score over our inner archenemy, ego, and its allies, the emotions. Within the manual, we shall find our interdimensional journey's history and our purpose in this experience. This code or record would be our Luminous DNA (see glossary), which is right beside our temporal biological history in the biological material DNA.

Decoded Contents of the Warrior of Light's Battle Manual

Before joining the battlefield, the Warrior must realize that:

1. Every Warrior is a son of the light and blood of his blood.

94

2.   Shadows are not his enemies, but slightly warmer shades of the light that complement his vision in his mirror-mind.

3.   Ego, attachment, and emotions are misinterpretations, created by newbie Warrior recruits that "still don't know what they're doing."

4.   The Warrior of Light's goal is not to wound the Warriors of Shadows, but rather to heal their self-inflicted emotional wounds with the balm of forgiveness to acknowledge their inner light.

5.   The Warrior of Light's arsenal is engraved in his luminous DNA, which can be found in the Akashic Records. The only thing he has to do is to decode it and remember it.

6.   He must know that the method to deal with emotions is to convert their goal and intentions with Love and not with selfishness, acknowledging they were self-created by our

ignorance.

7. Learn the positive opposite polarity of the
    emotion and try to use it as an exercise in
    willpower. This is part of the healing that arises
    from the previous steps. It's the loving effect of
    the law of cause and effect.

8. Acknowledge that spiritual relapses may be a
    part of the battle until we reach the level of
    Masters at Arms of the light.

9. Recognize that freedom from the prison created
    by the ego comes with the responsibility to
    decide the battle's outcome, since free will
    demands to be in control of the law of cause and
    effect, consciously using loving intention in every
    thought and word so that they may turn into
    actions full of light.

10. These realizations will lead them to a state of
    mental awareness where their mirror-mind's
    transparency will allow them to observe the

process of confusion with compassion, Love, and understanding.

11. Knowing ourselves through introspection with the courage to affect change but without judging. Watching ourselves in our mirror with Love and compassion so that other Warriors may do the same.

12. Acknowledge the spiritual crisis of the other Warriors in the battle. "Father, forgive them, for they do not know what they are doing." (Luke 23:34)

This journey's primary purpose is for the inner Warrior of Light to regain control of his cosmic destiny. From here on, the Warrior of Light turns into the Star of Peace, the Christ or the Buddha, having the capacity to help others recall their lineage and heal their emotional wounds.

After this process, the Warrior will recall the return code or coordinates to lead the time machine to his mind-mirror home.

The Arsenal of the Warrior of Light

He will have to discover all the weapons that reside potentially within his battle manual as the keys or medals he received for his victories are revealed, first in his inner battle and then fighting with other Warriors. The primary purpose is for him to learn first to recognize these weapons-attributes within himself, so that he may later accept them within the shadows of the other Warriors' Mirrors. In time, this will bestow upon him the knowledge, experience, and empathy to have the patience and compassion to learn. As we said initially, the weapons of the true Warrior of Light are compassion and the patience to wait for the other person to learn what he has already learned.

This is a list of the weapons that the Warrior has in his arsenal: Love (the origin) and its children:

knowledge, understanding, wisdom, solidarity, empathy, compassion, and patience.

All of them manifest as a result of the exploratory journey that begins with Love, to be later guided by solidarity in the tridimensional scale of space-time-matter.

In time, the Warrior shall have polished his mirror's surface so brightly that Warriors of Shadows that see themselves in it shall recognize their forgotten luminous attributes. This Warrior of Light will no longer see dragons and archetypal archenemies in his battles, but rather wounded Warriors of Shadows seeking the balm of forgiveness to heal their self-inflicted wounds.

The Composition of Our Human DNA

To understand the hypothesis I will posit regarding our DNA, we must review the description of the material and anti-material universe present in the first chapter of my first book, Spirituality 101: for the Dropouts of the School of Life. There, I described these two parts of the universe's characteristics and

99

proved that the material manifested in the tridimensional world of space-time occupied 5%. The anti-material multi-dimensional universe, outside time, occupied 95% of the total (see glossary).

Our DNA or deoxyribonucleic acid (Figure 1) is located in the nucleus of each cell of our bodies, where it is present as chromosomes with the genetic content organized in gene groups. Science has discovered that the organization of its contents determines all of the body's functional characteristics into genetic codes. This stored information is passed on to the new body in the reproductive process.

Junk DNA (Luminous DNA): The Unpolished Diamond that Exists Within Each Lump of Coal (Our Manual of The Warrior of Light)

Traditionally, the nucleus' genetic content is divided into a functional coding part occupying 3-5% and a non-functional or non-coding part termed "junk" for its cosmetic role, which paradoxically holds 95-97% of the total. Recent studies suggest that this junk DNA

100

is essential for influencing, activating, and deactivating coding functions in normal DNA. As other authors have suggested, lifestyles (emotional state, dietary habits, exercise, climate, etc.) might control junk DNA to modulate genetic functions in normal DNA. This phenomenon has been called Epigenetics (see glossary).

This branch of genetics studies how environmental factors can modify the pre-programmed function in the human genome. This has brought new hope for the control of genetic diseases and has created new treatment options. In later chapters, we will discuss how to use the epigenetic influence on our physical and spiritual health.

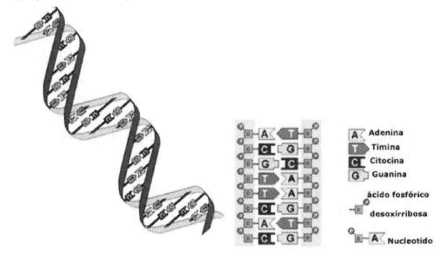

A — Adenina
T — Timina
C — Citocina
G — Guanina

ácido fosfórico
desoxirribosa

A — Nucleotido

DNA Structure - Our Universe Is Like the Material or Virtual Reflection Upon the Magical Mirror of Antimatter.

In line with the Warriors of Light and Shadows' similarities, the material universe may be described as the imperfect reflection of the Magical Mirror's anti-material universe. The Warrior of Shadows is an imaginary virtual creation caused by the Warrior of Light's nearsightedness and generated by the imperfections in his mirror's clarity. Science confirms this, establishing that the material universe originates from the anti-material one, though it cannot determine how this occurs.

The Material or Biological DNA and the Anti Material or Spiritual DNA Are Like Two Historical Scripts that Embrace In the Dance of Shiva with Creative (Yin) and Destructive (Yang) Rhythms to Ensure a Universal Harmonious Dance

These two historical archives of our multidimensional journey are those stored in the Universal Akashic Records (see glossary), that can

102

only be decoded by the veteran Warriors of the great battles of light, the Stars of Peace, or the Elders of the Great Brotherhood.

These records, codified in the Universal language, preserve all the Warriors' wisdom in their previous global campaigns. They bring when they return to their point of departure, the Magical Mirror-mind.

It's interesting to note that the ratio of the material world (5%) and the anti-material world (95%) is very similar to that of the coding DNA (3-5%) and the junk DNA (95-97%). Which could lead us to speculate: If we now know that junk DNA regulates the coding process of the rest of the DNA, could it be that the anti-material DNA is located there?

The Final Armistice of the Internal Battle

Then, after countless battles, the Warrior of Shadows joins forces with the Warrior of Light, in an armistice or cosmic quantum entanglement of Love and compassion, where the Star of Peace is born.

Some of these Warriors will return to the external battlefield as the Masters at Arms (see glossary) to help the Warriors of Shadows find their light.

Homework

Repeat the meditation from the previous chapter and learn to recognize the internal and external Warriors of Shadows' attributes. Observe the events that arouse good or bad qualities in them. Practice how the Warriors of Shadows respond to communications techniques of emotional intelligence or empathy, without seeking culprits or scapegoats. Allow yourself to make mistakes without criticizing yourself.

Bonus Questions

1. Might junk DNA be where the healing clues for the wounded Warriors of Light are found?

2. How do you think we can access these records?

104

CHAPTER V

THE WARRIOR'S EXTERNAL BATTLE: THE BATTLE OF THE EGOS

Description of the External Battlefront

That battlefront is the most dangerous of our two fronts, due to the countless amounts of Warriors of Shadows' distorted mirrors or egos to be found there. It feels like we're in an amusement park with the fun mirrors that amplify the reflection of our Warrior of Shadows' image thousands of times, disorienting and increasing the presence of our enemies.

It would seem that a lot of the imaginary shadows that we carry from our internal battlefront are projected upon other Warriors' mirrors on the battlefield, increasing their shadows.

The Warrior's Shadow Projects Even More as the Amount of His Emotional Wounds Increases.

As the emotional scars from the Warrior's external battle progress, so do the projections of his shadow and the light's obstruction in his mirror. That increase in his shadow allows him to darken other Warriors' mirrors with fear, increasing the enemy's army's reinforcements. That is why the Warrior of Light's tactics should not promote more negative emotions in the Warriors of Shadows because it only makes them more combative and dangerous.

Signs of an attack in the Battle Flanks

1. Progressive deterioration of the Warriors' physical health and general welfare, created by toxic lifestyles and promoted by the industries that profit from this situation (pharmaceutical, medical, and food). This leads to a dramatic increase in degenerative and congenital diseases in children and adults, cancer, and new diseases never previously seen. The toxic effects of these insults and our DNA manipulation could

106

cause nefarious epigenetic (see glossary) changes in our next generations.

2. Progressive deterioration in mental-emotional health resulting from the reasons mentioned above and the chronic stress state that frustration and anguish generate due to not having the requirements that the ego demands (for them to feel happy and fruitful). This problematic situation occurs due to social, racial, and economic disadvantages, or those imposed by the media, that hinder the Warrior from obtaining his happiness requirements. The worst part is that even those that get most of these achievements never attain happiness or achieve their welfare since the results do not fill the spiritual emptiness within them. The mighty ones that control the earthly experience use this to promote war, arguing that the Warriors' suffering is due to the enemy.

This incapacitating feeling leads many Warriors to crime, both blue and white-collar, and to the endless types of hallucinogenic and addictive drugs that destroy their minds-mirrors and make them fall deeper into their shadows, sometimes committing the distressing act of suicide.

The Four Flanks of the Warriors' External Battle

From their battle perimeter, the Warriors of Light find themselves defending four flanks, where they will face various enemy tactics:

1. The family front is on their frontal flank.

2. The school front is on their right flank.

3. Their work-professional front is on their left flank.

4. Their religious-spiritual front is at their rear.

In each of these flanks, the intensity of the battle fluctuates according to the size of the shadows that need to be enlightened. Their success will depend on the strength or capacity to successfully face confrontation in his frontal and rear flanks, where the lines are more prone to infiltration.

Stages of the Battle's Development

We must begin by remembering that the most powerful enemies focus their attack on the state of ignorance or innocence, created by our shadows' emotional blotches. They occur mainly in the early stages of training, or childhood, to battle in their familial and religious fronts. Depending on the degree of light or shadows exhibited by their Masters at Arms, these new Warriors will develop the attributes needed to lighten or darken the enemy Warriors' mirror-minds.

Therefore, the quality of our Masters at Arms on these two flanks can guide our destinies towards light or shadows. Even if our Masters at Arms still do not command the techniques for irradiating their light in a specific battle, other good Samaritans will always turn up, also Masters at Arms. The latter can help us activate our inner Warrior of Light.

The Family Flank and Its Influence on the Warriors

This first phase of the external battle exerts the most significant influence on our capacity for victory since it determines the possible tactical knowledge we'll bring to our battlefront. The law of cause and effect has a significant impact on this flank.

The law of cause and effect, free will, and intention can create "heavens" or "hells" in our battlefronts. To better understand the law of love, we could state that "the cause would be the light, and the effect would be the shadow."

Loving Intention and Selfish Intention: The Cause Behind our Battlegrounds

Our inherent right from the beginning of our exploratory voyage has been and will be to have free will, which allowed us to reproduce the creative capacity of the Big Bang and the resulting Magical Mirror, but which includes the responsibility for the result generated by our intention. As we have already

110

discussed, free will in deciding our destinations or battlegrounds varies according to our light's capacity or purity to distinguish all the resulting consequences in the Warriors' entire holographic matrix.

The farther a Warrior strays from his point of departure, the more he forgets or disconnects his light and universal language, and the image in his mirror-mind darkens even further. But the Warrior that possesses a loving intention stemming from his light never disconnects and understands that his shadows are but magical shades of his light.

The emotional effect is like diminishing night vision, where emotions are like the other car's high beams. We will have a lessened perspective regarding the results created by his intentions. Still, more options to choose from, without being aware of his action's effects upon the other Warriors in the voyage. Again, this reminds me of Jesus' quote, "Father, forgive them, for they do not know what they are doing." (Luke 23:34). But we must remember that the law of cause and effect, in a fair way, does not exempt you from the consequences of your ignorant actions.

Universal Intention Is Based on Love (We, Ours), While Global Intention Is Based on Selfishness and Individualism (Me, Mine)

Universal Intention

It relies on a vision of an interdependent universe, interwoven with a holographic matrix of love, like when the musical harmony of the cosmic symphony is more important than the musicians and their instruments.

This implies that, as the Warriors progress in their journey's multidimensional experiences, their free will has a fuller array of options to decide, but with less capacity to see the consequences.

Global Intention

A global intention is one of the goals that Warriors must attain on their way back to their point of departure to develop the "intention" as solar, galactic,

112

and finally universal beings. We can divide the global intention into geographical, national, racial, religious, political, economic, and gender-based areas.

These classes are based on each group's interests, causing confrontational conflicts to a greater or lesser degree due to their particular or selfish inclinations. Many of these differences brought social or political movements that caused wars, with catastrophic results for the parties and the planet. Warriors' interactions on these levels generate endless chains of cause and effect, creating bad experiences for several generations.

The Processes in Our Family Battlefront

The family battlefront can be the most combative and confusing of all, since our worst "enemies" may be found here. To better understand how to deal with the other Warriors on this front, we must observe how our DNA influences it.

On this Front, Our Family Makes it Difficult for Us to Recognize Our True Enemy; The Biological DNA

To understand this lineage paradox, we must recall that before incarnating in this material tridimensional universe, we all come from a shared lineage or family, light, and love, which gave birth to us in the reflection of the Magical Mirror. As we descended through the different stops in our interdimensional voyage, we forgot our shared lineage and our light's purity, which generated the false perception of our shadows as our actual reality.

When the Warrior of Light arrives at the tridimensional destination of space-time, the mind-mirror, almost entirely darkened by its disconnection from its center of light, creates a deformed imitation of the immortal luminous DNA with its free will. This was the biological, material, or mortal DNA which, to keep on reproducing, produces birth, death, and sexual reproduction to perpetuate itself. Since then, the legacies of the Warrior of Light and the Warrior of

Shadows have lived in a binary state in the family battleground. The Warrior of Shadows lives entirely ruled by the law of cause and effect and by its concomitant cycle of rebirth, disease, and death, described in the Oriental traditions.

The Influence of Biological Genetics on their Progeny - The Sins of the Parents Up Until the Fourth Generation

Let's analyze this passage from Exodus 20:5, "You shall not bow down to them or worship them; for I, the Lord your God, am a jealous God, punishing the children for the sin of the parents to the third and fourth generation of those who hate me."

This passage made me very angry in my youth, as per the "injustice" that God's justice implied. But revisiting it in light of our new dual concept of DNA, it would seem to be very reasonable.

Genetic science and epigenetics explain the effect on future generations. We know that genetic changes can arise due to mutations, negative or

115

positive, and be passed on to the progeny during sexual reproduction. Many of these genetic influences appeared in previous generations as congenital disabilities, metabolic disorders, tendencies towards particular types of cancers, chromosomal disorders, etc. We also know that alcoholism, schizophrenia, bipolar syndrome, and psychopathy can have some genetic roots.

If we also include that epigenetics can structurally and functionally modify biological DNA, we will understand that "sins" mean "lifestyles" in the biblical passage. The important part is that lifestyles include emotional effects, such as negative emotions and toxins acquired by the five senses (what we see, hear, think, say, touch, and eat), influencing our genome's quality. Thus, the importance of the state of health and parents' mental attitude during the conception of a new Warrior. Remember that the Warriors of Light who want to join our Warriors of Shadows need a conducive environment.

Epigenetic Influence - The Upbringing Environment

The power of the positive impact of lifestyles over our genome's activity and genetic makeup fills us with the hope of improving our biological DNA to create new health paradigms in our future generations. This will allow for better synchronization between our two DNAs to pacify the Warriors' battles. If we can, under the influence of our luminous DNA, awaken and manifest the light, mitigating the emotional wounds in the Warriors of Shadows, our intentions, guided by the light, will produce fewer "hells" and more heavens in our lives.

Influence of Spiritual Genetics

This is identical to the Warrior of Light's purpose, as discussed in previous chapters:

The Warrior of Light's goal in battle is to free the light within the Warrior of Shadows, activating his forgiveness code, which is like Windex for his mirror, helping him heal his emotional wounds so that he may shine his mirror to eliminate all the impurities that do not let him see its light. This Warrior does not believe in the force of confrontation but rather in logic, understanding, commitment, and forgiveness, and has infinite patience to achieve it.

As discussed in previous chapters, you must recall that the Warrior of Shadows' internal battles and his victories brought medals in the form of codes that work like keys to decipher the healing codes in the luminous DNA. This allows the Warrior to learn new light tactics to use them in his external battlefield (family, religious, work-related, political, etc.).

Examples of external battles that make it easy for us to carry out the Warrior of Light's purpose:

Family Front

1. Child raising in dysfunctional families

2. Extreme poverty

3. Sex and child abuse

4. Divorces

5. Diseases in children and parents

6. Orphanhood

7. Use of recreational drugs

8. Criminality

9. Codependent relationships

Religious Front

1. Religious repression

2. Birth control

3. Child abuse

4. Manipulation of salvation concepts/religious codependency

5. Religious fanaticism

6. Proselytism

Educational Front

1. Racial and gender discrimination

2. Economic and social injustice in education

3. Educational systems based on the prejudice and selfishness of the powerful, and with financial goals

4. An educational system that indoctrinates, and does not promote intellectual creativity

5. An educational system that encourages exclusive rights to knowledge over what benefits the society of Warriors

Health Front

1. Turns health into a business.

2. Health guarantee equals financial capacity.

3. Pharmaceutical companies dictate therapeutic procedures and profit from their sales.

4. The pharmaceutical industry controls medical

education, motivated not by the promotion of health and prevention, but rather to prolong the disease that maintains the supply and demand relationship. Why is there a progressive increase in degenerative conditions and cancer while health budgets increase?

5. Medical education favors those who can afford it.

6. The medical practice in control hounds complementary and traditional medical practices.

7. Progressive increase in dependence on prescription drugs.

Economic and Political Front

1. Economic oppression, where 90% of the economy is in 10% of the population.

2. The exploitation of manual labor in poorer countries.

121

3. The irresponsible exploitation of our planet's natural resources: oil, minerals, water, timber, animals.

4. Air, water, and land pollution with toxic substances.

5. The persistent increase in famine in poorer countries.

6. Increased criminality and corruption at all social and political levels.

7. Persistence of totalitarian and religious political regimes.

Hand to Hand Combat Techniques to Be Victorious in the External Battlefield

1. Do not reply with emotional weapons, since emotions (good or bad) can be instruments of love or weapons of subtle but massive destruction.

2. Don't reply with your shadow to the Warrior of Shadows; respond with your Light to discover his own.

3. Transmute your negative emotions

    a) Accept that they were created by our actions due to ignorance, without blaming ourselves because we did not know what we were doing.

    b) Learn the positive opposite polarity of the emotion and try to use it as an exercise in willpower. This applies during mindfulness meditation.

    c) Learn to know yourself by seeing yourself courageously, but without judging. Learn to see yourself in your mirror with love and compassion so that everyone else follows your example.

    d) Learn to transform obsolete programming with

willpower, using the Golden Rule: Do not do unto others what you would not want to be done to yourself.

e) Acknowledge that every transformation brings a spiritual healing crisis, created by the preceding steps, which always bears fruit.

f) Acknowledge that spiritual relapses are part of the battle. Sometimes we take two steps forward and three steps back, and vice versa, but in the end, we see that summing up, we have progressed. Don't think you are perfect since you could not see your light without your shadows.

g) Be responsible in your use of thought, word, and action. Freedom from the ego's prison generates the responsibility of deciding the battle's outcome. True free will demands to control the law of cause and effect, consciously using every thought, word, and action.

4. The preceding will lead them to a state of mental awareness where their mirror-mind's transparency will allow them to observe with knowledge, understanding, love, and compassion, which creates the patience to wait for the dissolution of the confusion of the other Warriors in the battle.

5. Afterward, the inner Warrior of Light has regained control of his cosmic destiny. From here on, the Warrior of Light turns into the Star of Peace, the Christ or the Buddha, having the capacity to endlessly help others recall their lineage and heal, recovering their light.

6. After this process, the Warrior will remember or decode the return coordinates to lead the time machine of his mind-mirror home.

Homework

1. Repeat the Warrior's Oath.

2. Repeat the mindfulness meditation, regarding how your day went in the different battlefields. Identify where it is the weakest and needs more reinforcements.

3. Set up partnerships with Warriors or Masters at Arms to obtain new victories and tactics for every front or flank. Do not try to do battle on all flanks at the same time.

Bonus Questions

1. Examine how intention can support or hinder your progress and victories. Do not reply with the enemy's same weapons and tactics.

2. What are your strongest habits or your darkest shadows? Which ones can you use to substitute them?

3. Why do the weapons of the Warriors of Shadows within our family setting inflict the most severe wounds? (Note: It's related to the ego,

attachment, and the concept of a biological and spiritual family.)

CHAPTER VI

UNIVERSAL LANGUAGE OF THE MAGICAL MIRROR: THE WARRIOR OF LIGHT'S SUPPLY AND COMMUNICATIONS LINES

The fruitful outcome of the battles and wars markedly depends on weapons, food, and human reinforcement supply lines being better than those of the enemy. In the case of the supreme command of the Warriors of Shadows' army, as they are not connected to the Magical Mirror, they can only resupply from deserters of the Warriors of Light, using tactics that disturb their emotional states.

On the other side, the supreme command of the Warriors of Light has an inexhaustible supply of resources available through the universal language's communications channels, encoded with the symbols of light. The key that translates this language into our dialect is stored within the luminous DNA, and only veteran Warriors, who have triumphed both in their internal and external battles, can open the supply lines, as they clean up the distortions reflected by their mirrors.

The Universal Language Written with the Alphabet of Love

Love is the universal language, which allows the self to recall its spiritual origins by acknowledging in the reflection of his Magical Mirror that his companions in battle in the school of life belong to his lineage (blood of his blood). The languages that appear later during the interdimensional exploration process are the infinite dialects that arise from the endless forms in which we interpret and manifest love in our lives.

These linguistic variants originate from the level of comprehension, or battle experience, in which we find ourselves in our combat experience. For example, the socioeconomic scale, health status, sectarian

130

religious belief, and genetic inheritance all influence his psycho-social experience.

Wisdom is learning to recognize the roots of our collective tongue, love, and having enough patience to learn to understand all of them during their military life experience in all of these guttural variants.

I wish that your experience while reading this book provides the tools so that love always guides your thoughts, and your thoughts drive your words, and both direct your actions.

The Differences Between the Alphabet of the Universal Language and That of the Other Dialects

To understand these differences, you must realize that, as the traveler-Warrior moves away from his point of departure, and the voyage experiences and knowledge multiplies, the traveler will have more information to classify and file away in his logbook (luminous DNA and material DNA). As these are entirely new experiences, he will have to create new words and definitions for them.

Since many travelers are experiencing and filing away many experiences, different interpretations of the same experience will duplicate, creating communication gaps between the various languages. This will separate the Warriors even more into clans, races, and countries, with their particular religious, social, and political beliefs.

This experience's subjectivity will make it imperative to increase the number of words needed to describe the same observation during the trip, complicating the capacity to broadcast the message even more. That difference can be rapidly noted while observing how the original message changes during its translation to another language and when we try to translate jokes.

The universal language that describes the state of awareness at the beginning of the journey had fewer words or symbols that described the universal

132

experience more inclusively without the ambivalence of emotional polarity, which shows up later in the new destinations. This was the language that many sages described in their philosophical treatises.

The Symbols in Ancient Philosophical Treatises: Plato's Archetypes

While reviewing this and other topics great philosophers studied, I regret not having paid the necessary attention to my college humanities classes! Plato, the same as the Buddha, described a dual universe, divided into the material, real, or relative, where we live and classify with our five senses and its subjective nature, and the transcendental, absolute, or anti-material, where ideas or archetypes lie in a dormant state.

In the transcendental, the self has access to creating, with the proper technique, all possible manifestations of each archetype in reality. From our modern scientific viewpoint, it is understood that all events that occurred and are occurring after the Big

133

Bang are the archetypes or symbols that we, Warriors of Light, will later have to discover and classify in the real world. Each symbol abstracts and includes itself, as if it were a memory chip of Light, an infinite amount of ideas to decode and create.

To understand this more clearly, let us take the Tai Chi symbol as an example (see illustration):

This symbol is an archetype of every action's dual nature, which manifests in opposing forces and recurring cycles. The dark part represents the absence of light, coldness, femininity, passivity, and the centripetal force (that unites, attracts, reaps). The white region represents the light, heat, masculinity, activity, the centrifugal force (that which separates, repels, sows). The opposing color spheres symbolize that the opposite is always potentially within its counterpart, ready to manifest as the cycle, time, or sinusoidal line favors it.

This archetype harbors many ideas, like maternity, paternity, climate cycles, chemical and physical reactions, agricultural production cycles, the physiological cycles of biological organisms, mental creativity, etc. If we understand all that is abstracted in this archetype, we can create new and infinite ideas for our material experience.

Pythagoras' Music of the Spheres

Pythagoras postulated that numbers, combinations, and sequences included keys or symbols, whose organization composed a musical harmony that ruled the universe and its planets like a universal symphony. That explains the resonance between the stars and biological organisms. Accessing these musical symbols can help Warriors replenish their reserves during their battles.

Every Warrior of Light must visualize his role within the universe as essential, but not unique. His participation in the cosmic symphony must not focus on the instrument or how extensive his involvement is, but instead on how, without his part, the symphony would be incomplete and dissonant.

Sacred Geometry: The Symbolic Alphabet of the Universal Language

My interpretation of this philosophy is that the keys and symbols that Pythagoras spoke of are archetypes of geometry like the original alphabet of the universal language, created with the primordial intelligence of the Magical Mirror. These symbols encompass the creative ideas interwoven by the force of love and embedded in our genetic code, or luminous DNA since the beginning of the universe. We can see an example of this in the mandalas created by Tibetan monks and crop circles worldwide. These are another

136

source to provide the supplies of the Warrior of Light's army.

Methods to Open Communications with these Sources of Reinforcements for Our Light

The essential key is activating the memory of all of these archetypal symbols (sacred geometry) of our universal language that resides in our luminous DNA.

1. Receive medals in both battlefronts: With each victory, the Warrior keeps polishing his mirror-mind's surface and starts progressively recalling and seeing his light. This starts to decode serial sections of his luminous DNA, strengthening his battle strategy in the external perimeter where the reflection of his light progressively convinces other Warriors of the Shadows to acknowledge their light and join his side.

2. Understand his responsibility in creating his imaginary battles with his archenemy, the ego, due to the adverse emotional reactions that allowed him to cloud the true reflection of the

137

light in this mirror-mind. The self-forgiveness of this action is what facilitates the activation of his healing codes.

3. This forgiveness arises from the comprehension, empathy, patience, and compassion, which allow him to see that each tactical error and defeat in battle comes from ignorance, by not perceiving his inner light due to the emotional nearsightedness created by his emotional wounds. This exonerates him from all intentional blame, without eliminating his responsibility for correcting his tactical errors.

4. In the teachings of the Buddha and Jesus, they emphasized that every wrong action occurs because of the Warrior's limited vision or ignorance in recognizing his inner light. We can find that in the following quotes: Jesus', "Father, forgive them, for they do not know what they are doing" (Luke 23:34), and Buddha's, "The difference between a Buddha and a vile criminal

is that the criminal still hasn't realized that he is a Buddha."

5. With his new weapons of knowledge, understanding, compassion, love, and forgiveness, the Warrior can nullify the effects of the Warrior of Shadows' weapons: emotions, selfishness, attachment, and ambition and help others recognize their light.

6. Maintaining a state of alert, thus avoiding contamination with the energies of darkness in our external battlefield: home, work, schools, advertising media, and toxic lifestyles. The shadows' command center uses the communications media, the food industry, educational centers, the industrial financial-military power, religious structures, and the health industry to program the Warrior of Light's mind-mirror (see preceding paragraph). So maintaining a state of alert for the watchmen on our flanks is a battle priority. In other chapters,

we will delve more deeply into the techniques we can use towards this end.

7. This activation process is facilitated by creating partnerships with other Warriors of Light in all our flanks: family, work, religious and educational, that support our efforts. As the saying goes, "You will be judged by the company you keep." Likewise, we must read books that help activate our codes of light in our DNA. We must also observe spiritual lifestyles that govern how we relate to others in our homes, workplaces, and religious and political organizations. And not poison our bodies with junk food, alcoholic beverages, medicines, drugs, electromagnetic fields, lack of exercise, unbridled sexuality, discordant music, and toxic communications media.

Homework

1. Let's repeat the Warrior's Oath and the past day's mindfulness meditation. Let's go over how

we establish the quality of communications at all levels of Warriors and battlefronts.

2. Let's review how we can recall or decipher our DNA's universal language.

Bonus Questions

1. Why is it impossible to communicate with purity and clarity in the tridimensional material experience? (It has to do with the light that allows me to see my mirror with fewer cloudiness prejudices, mental programs, chips, etc.)

2. Review Plato's theory of archetypes in this chapter.

CHAPTER VII

LOVE IS LIKE THE IMAGES REFLECTED IN A DIAMOND'S FACETS, CREATED BY THE EGO'S EMOTIONAL NEARSIGHTEDNESS

"If You Can't Find Love Around You, It Is Because You Still Haven't Searched Inside Yourself."

The voyage and experiences learned in battle polish the porous surfaces of coal to reflect all of the hidden light that has always been inside it.

In this chapter, I try to observe the Magical Mirror's turbulent and emotionally charged reflections in a more precise way, hoping to attain a more compassionate view of love. To achieve this, we must set off on a historic voyage.

The Traditional Meaning of Love

Love is a smoke raised with the fume of sighs;

Being purged, a fire sparkling in lovers' eyes;

Being vexed, a sea nourished with loving tears.

What is it else? A madness most discreet,

A choking gall and a preserving sweet.

(Shakespeare)

This is the true measure of love:

when we believe that we alone can love,

that no one could ever have loved so before us,

and that no one will ever love in the same way

after us.

(Johann Wolfgang von Goethe)

Love as a Cause of Illnesses

According to ancient medical writers, symptoms produced when passion is an illness are: fluttering eyelids, sunken eyes yet seemingly full of pleasure, and the peculiar pulse of passion. As the force of love prevails, symptoms seem to become more evident: a tremor that affects heart and pulse, loss of appetite, agitated fever, melancholy, or perhaps dementia, if not death, make up the sad catastrophe. (A description of "Love in Medicine," according to the Encyclopaedia Britannica Thesaurus, 1788.)

The Many Expressions or Reflections of Love

We could infinitely quote the different meanings of love without satisfying anyone on this planet, or in the very Universe. Let us then try to find a standard definition for the manifestations of love. Intrinsically, all descriptions of love in this tridimensional world include three components in their formula: a subject (the lover), an object (the beloved), and the act of "loving." The object may be a subject or a person, but it can also be a thing such as a book, a hobby, a pet, money, or power.

As we analyze this triangular relationship, the subject feels the right to possess the object of his love, which gives him a feeling of satisfaction depending on the subjective value assigned to the object by the subject that "loves it." If we accept the love triangle's analogy as an interdependent one, both the subject and the object experience feelings. All components of the equation share the same levels of satisfaction. We must conclude that a real love relationship has to have a certain degree of reciprocity. At least we believe that when entering into a relationship!

Feeling satisfied and well by possessing things is something very personal. Still, if the object owned is something material, it cannot "feel" the attachment that the person who "possesses" feels, and neither can it respond. Therefore, things like cars, sports, and books cannot love us, but we can feel loved by the mental processes that these objects evoke in us. This usually happens when we recall past moments in our lives when we felt loved. Based on this nearsighted concept of love, traditional experience divides love into four groups: romantic, economic, or of supply and demand, maternal or familial, and religious.

146

Romantic Love

This type of love evolved with the rise of complex societies and social classes (remember the loss of the universal language), cultural inequalities in wealth and education, and influence upon chivalry and virginal purity concepts. That was a long time ago! Literary and religious influences promoted all of this. In primitive societies, wedding vows had practical, social, economic, and political guidelines that did not account for women's needs. This has not changed much! Women are treated as property, without their legal rights.

In some traditional societies, women were betrothed to their husbands at a very young age, pushed towards motherhood and roles they were unfamiliar with. Therefore, Romanticism is a literary concept that initially influenced noblemen to establish specific "rules of conduct" based on religious traditions. Those traditions eventually referenced the objects of their respect, the pure women of their dreams, for whom they could sacrifice their lives in

147

defense of their honor. The arrival of democratic governments and the advancement of the struggles for women's rights during the last two centuries kept somewhat promoting this vision of love in society.

Economic Love - Supply and Demand

In the past, only the wealthy and aristocratic classes had an advantage when the moment came to obtain the favors of the opposite sex, ensuring the continuity of the bloodline. But even in those turbulent times, aristocratic lineages were less important than economic and political power. The freedoms and rights obtained by women and the gender equity movements have changed how women see themselves. However, many men still have a medieval mentality, creating conflicting opinions about modern women.

Love has turned into a marketable good, defined by the latest advertising that sells things, so people feel loved and adorable. Men and women act and look in particular ways to ensure their allotment of love. This "free market" concept leads love down a risky

148

path, which ends exclusively in sex. Traditional families are disappearing and with them, the birthrate in most industrial societies. The divorce index is higher than the stock exchange, and attorneys are the only ones benefiting from that crisis. Many modern couples marry for convenience, to raise their children before a certain age, or for tax incentives. This situation reminds me of Tina Turner's song, "What's love got to do with it?"

There's a love that arises from the physical union from the procreative act; we always marvel at seeing a birth, be it human or animal. This has an archetypal influence (triangle, Yin-Yang, electron-proton) upon the emergence of life in this Universe. We see it as an instinct to protect offspring in most animal kingdom females. This highly idealized love is influenced by religious opinions, where the feminine principle is sacred. The power of romantic literature also fosters this type of love. The most prominent feature of this love is the generosity or sacrifice of the mother's needs before that of the child.

Sadly, this innate instinct of nearly all animals in the initial rearing stages is not seen automatically in all the human race's mothers. It varies according to the mother's experience with her family, her personality and mental balance, dictated by their emotional battle wounds. We only need to study the incidence of mistreatment and child abuse that modern societies experience to understand that love does not show in all mothers equally. Some are overwhelmed by their shadows.

Religious Love

Though the theological interpretation of love may vary between religions, most are theocentric (God is the creator) and panentheistic (God is beyond his creation), contrasting with pantheism, where God is a part of his creation. This love's initial concept says that all love comes from the principle of one God. It is only obtainable through "him," with different theological guidelines established by the respective religions' ecclesiastical hierarchy.

150

That co-dependent relationship, spiritually blind and pathological, influences how humans perceive love between themselves. That love tends to ask the believer to love all beings generously, imitating God's actions, without considering the believer's needs or ability to achieve it.

The True Nature of Love

To understand the meaning of love, I will reference my first book, "Spirituality 101: For the Dropouts of the School of Life," and compare that vision regarding spirituality vs. traditional religious concepts.

Starting from the scientific perspective, where antimatter originates matter and comparing the corresponding attributes that emerge from both parts of the duality, spiritual and religious, you may establish the table that defines and compares these characteristics, which I will shortly recap. Though our initial awareness regarding the nature of love in the Universe's creative process was the Big Bang, love lives in the passive silence whence the Big Bang originated.

We must humbly understand that the ephemeral and tridimensional state we call "human reality" is an insignificant component in a Universe that may hypothetically have up to twelve dimensions. For some mysterious reason, this multidimensional and majestic origin of our spiritual-antimatter Universe got disconnected from its tridimensional offspring: religion-matter. This results in alienated life experiences, independent of their source.

Knowledge Ruled by Reason and Logic, and the Five Physical Senses

In my first book, I called this troubling feeling of the self "cosmic schizophrenia," and I call it "battle-originated schizophrenia" in this one. It's a state of mental confusion that stems from this dual division's philosophical and religious interpretations. If we accept my explanation regarding our origins, we realize that these "spiritual" attributes reside interdependently in our Universe's dimensional levels and conscious participants. They are qualities inherent in all that is involved in creation.

These fundamental characteristics that existed before the Big Bang manifested later as the famous "Bang," and then as all the different dimensional forms that exist today, joined in a maternal matrix that reflects everything in a mirror of Love. This is what I believe is spiritual love. This is the love that all of the great masters of all religions have tried to explain, but the founders of sectarian religious organizations didn't get it. These "founders" built human-made bridges to reconnect humans with their source of light, but those bridges controlled by gates with sectarian tolls only "filter" those who can use them.

Spiritual Love, the Hidden Diamond in each Lump of Coal

The potential state intrinsic to all living beings that are aware in the creative process is like the lump of coal that awaits the alchemical power of love to

153

transform into a magnificently bright diamond, hidden in the reflection of each of its facets. This magical phenomenon can only happen when we observe the brilliant attributes in those who have polished their mirrors to different perfection levels.

Then the process of love is finding hidden treasures in your yard by observing others discover theirs. A more poetic way to see this is that we are like mirrors, with the capacity to reflect the nature and quality of our brightness or love, so that others can learn to recognize the rough diamond they carry in their hearts. That implies that the purity of each person's crystal's reflection varies according to their understanding, the one obtained through life's experience.

At some moments, our past experiences can, inappropriately, provoke fearful memories in our minds, obstructing our capacity to attain the bright nature or our pure diamond, thus forestalling those hidden qualities from being recognized by others. This

154

generates an imaginary protective wall, which also blurs our sight, preventing us from recognizing the love in those who share our life. That creates a feeling of separation, loneliness, and emptiness that we can never satisfy with material things. That sense of lack of love can only be mitigated when we let go of our fear and tear down our imaginary wall in the face of love.

Ironically, sometimes the real experiences of suffering that raise our defenses are the ones that lead our Soul to open anew. This allows our heart to see our magnificent crystal again, as reflections in other beings' mirror. These suffering experiences often synchronize our heart in a big and compassionate hug of forgiveness with others who are undergoing similar situations. The lack of this understanding darkens our inner diamond's natural brightness, like the deposits that appear in precious stones when not maintained with regular cleanings.

The Many Facets of Love Reflect Infinite Paradigms

For convenience, we tend to divide love into distinct types. All the facets that reflect it's brightness are infinite models according to the quality of their reflections in our Universe's mirror. All of these variables are necessary to allow the presence of love in each person's experiences.

All of these experiences join in the infinite patience of spiritual love. Thus, love is a constant learning process that slowly polishes the brightness of the intrinsic purity of our hearts' diamond and allows us to select its light rays in the mirrors of the others. Therefore, in any love relationship, love is not "given," nor "lost," no one can "break" our heart, and when the connection is over, each takes with him/her all of the love awoken in the process. This vision of love must create awareness of the fact that we create the experience of suffering due to our confusion. Can we then agree with the song's title, "What's love got to do with it?"

156

With the following quote, I sum up the vision of love that the Warrior of Light must wield during his experience in battle.

When the Warrior looks at the universe in the reflection of his Magical Mirror, he only sees infinite numbers of wounded Warriors of Light, waiting to receive the balm of forgiveness to heal their emotional wounds.

Homework

1. God made us to create a massive epidemic of love in his creation. What have you done today to infect others? Don't misuse your time sharing your fears.

2. Learn to recognize the brightness of your diamond by acknowledging it first in that of others.

3. Show others your diamond so that they recognize your light and learn to polish their diamond.

4. To achieve the goals mentioned above, do the Warrior of Light meditation and keep practicing the "back to the future" exercise of forgiveness later in the book.

Bonus Questions

1. Observe what you feel when you see others' diamonds shining more than yours. Envy, jealousy, anger, disappointment, joy, hope, illusion, motivation?

2. Where do negative and positive emotions come from?

3. What can you do to eliminate the negative and foster the positive? (Suggestion: revise the concepts of quantum entanglement, the origin of the ego and emotions.)

CHAPTER VIII

HEALING THE WOUNDS OF THE WARRIOR OF LIGHT; FIRST AID KIT FOR THE BATTLEFRONT

Forgiveness: The Warrior's Healing Balm

Forgiveness can instantaneously heal the Warrior's wounds if, during his battles, he has acquired the knowledge, understanding, and empathy to have compassion and patience for his defeats and those of other Warriors in their multidimensional voyage.

Using the tactics and combat weapons of the Warriors of Shadows only increases the ranks of enemy soldiers and the number of new battles, due to the law of cause and effect.

Forgiveness is the secret weapon that neutralizes the forces of the army of shadows with light and love.

159

Don't reply with your shadow to the Warriors of Shadows, answer with your light so that you may help him discover his own.

The following poem sums up very well the meaning of forgiveness:

THE MELODIOUS SILENCE OF THE COSMOS

Silence yearns to quench the Soul's unending thirst for Love,

yet in its splendor, it fails to stifle the continuous yet fleeting chatter of the ego;

for the Soul has long forgotten its majestic tranquility.

How will I be able, then, to arouse the remembrance of its melodious song again?

I have already realized that this will not occur by increasing the volume of the dissonant notes of my mundane life.

Nor by recalling the memories of my frivolous experiences,

which only ignite more the flames of my insatiable desire for them,

those infernal passions that muted even more my sense of hearing.

How can I stifle then the deafening shame of the condemning voices that punish my heart?

Perhaps only by realizing that all my lapses were committed with the innocence of intention,

and stipulated by the ignorance of my divine lineage.

Clearly established by our great Teacher, Jesus, who in his last words said,

161

"Father, forgive them, for they do not know what they are doing." (Luke 23:34)

My heart then finally finds peace, as I understand that in the forgiveness of my transgressions,

and those done to me by others,

resides the final solution to my paradox.

And then, suddenly, a thunderous emptiness permeates every corner of my Universe,

reawakening in my heart the Melodious Silence Of The Cosmos.

The Luminous Contents of the Warrior of Light's First Aid Kit

1. "First, know thyself." This phrase was required for initiates to enter the School of Mysteries of the Temple of Delphi and applies to the Warrior of Light when he decides to seek his reflection in

his mirror-mind. Though the Warrior must always find his light, he should not ignore the shadows that he created with his emotions, since the solution to finding his light lies within them. Fighting with your shadows can, like it did to Don Quixote with his windmills, lead you to mental instability if you do not accept that they are like dragons invented by your imagination run amok by your emotions and your ego.

2. Don't begin an imaginary battle with the rules of engagement and objectives of a real one if you don't want to lose it, and use the tactics discussed in previous chapters regarding our internal and external battlefronts. Remember that replying to attacks from the Warriors of Shadows with their weapons only increases your emotional battle wounds and increase the ranks of the Warriors of Shadows.

3. The reflective wisdom of the Magical Mirror is the self-esteem that the Master at Arms manifests

after his many victories in the battles during his voyage, rendering him a steady source of wisdom due to the knowledge, understanding, empathy, and compassion that he has acquired. This is the Warrior who is grateful for the help from other Masters at Arms who helped him in his battles and joyously commits to assisting other warriors in their battles. Some quotes he has learned from his mirror are:

Don't reply with your shadow to the Warriors of Shadows, answer with your light so that you may help him discover his own.

If you can't find love around you, you still haven't looked inside yourself.

Emotions can be instruments of love or weapons of mass destruction.

Remember that every Warrior of Light is always with his shadow and that without it, he could never recognize his light.

Paradoxically, our shadows seem more prominent when we approach the light.

4. Don't join deserters from your side, who want to form co-dependent alliances as if they were spiritually lame. They only want to use you as a crutch, to shirk their responsibility in the battlefield and grab the medals you deserve. We often find these deserters in our familial battle flank. Long term, they drain you of all that you need to be victorious in battle.

5. Always seek the most advantageous strategic location in combat, which will help you reflect your Light upon the enemy to force him to surrender without losing a single Warrior of Shadows. Using a heart full of compassion as the negotiating table, you can nearly always get a dignified and fair armistice.

6. Never corner the enemy, since this will only force him to defend himself more aggressively, like a cat trapped by a dog. Show him your light

with the compassionate act of allowing him a dignified withdrawal, then negotiate a truce where he does not lose face since you have also tasted the bitterness of defeat.

7.   Never eschew an ambushed battle, since the intensity or courage with which you employ your light will awaken your enemy's courage and light.

8.   Do not abandon nor deny help to a wounded Warrior of Shadows, since your courage and compassion could heal his emotional wounds and awaken his light.

9.   Do not deny your first aid to injured Warriors of Shadows. Remember that they were Warriors of Light and that their emotional wounds have clouded the light in their mirror-minds. They are living in the confusion of their ignorance, for they know not what they do.

10. Forgiveness is the balm of light that heals all battlefront wounds since it treats the Warrior that bestows it and the one that receives it.

The Wound Formation Process

To understand the healing mechanism, we must study how wounds happen. We must realize that these are self-inflicted by the adverse and uncontrolled emotional reaction that the Warrior generates when he feels suffering (review chapters I and II). These wounds do not heal appropriately due to the infections that external organisms create: attachment, anger, guilt, frustration, hate, resentment, envy, and other emotions that are plentiful on the battlefield and infect wounds. The tendency to blame others for our battle experiences and injuries amplifies the effect of infectious emotions.

As these infections progress, they further cloud the Warrior's mirror-mind, plunging him into a hideous gloom of inexplicable neglect and suffering, leading him to psychiatric problems, depressions, and addictions criminality, and even suicide. In these advanced cases, several therapies could aid in his rehabilitation.

Healing Techniques

You can find information about these methods that we shall mention without detailed explanations in the communications media. They all stem from the concept that emotions are stored with their harmful code, negatively influencing physical welfare, even creating physical symptoms. Its effects are not as useful as self-healing, which we will discuss at the end of the chapter.

1. Traditional psychology

2. Transpersonal psychology is a therapeutic approach aimed at having human beings achieve optimal welfare and psychological help, highlighting modifications of states of awareness beyond the limits of ego and personality. It connects psychology with spirituality, seeking man's self-realization and self-transcendence.

168

3. Ho'oponopono (ho-oh-ponoh-ponoh) is a very ancient Hawaiian art of problem resolution based on reconciliation and forgiveness. The original Hawaiians, the islands' first inhabitants, used to practice it. Morrnah Nalamaku Simeona (May 19, 1913 - February 11, 1992) brought us these teachings and updated them for modern times. Nowadays, they are used by practitioners and therapists from different disciplines.

4. Therapies to unload emotions

   a) NLP - Neurolinguistic programming- "It's a model about how our mind works, how this affects language and how to use it to program ourselves in the sense of making our lives and the things we do easier more efficient at the same time," Robert Dilts. Though most practitioners are psychologists, this is not a pre-requisite to study it. It has several variants to discharge and heal emotions.

   b) Clinical hypnosis- Practiced by physicians,

169

non-physicians, and psychologists, can heal past emotional wounds.

c) Hypnotic regression therapy - Though it is used to treat emotional experiences that allegedly originate in past lives, some use it for regressions in this life.

I. Somato Emotional Release - It's a therapeutic variant of craneo-sacral therapies that rid the mind and body of the residual effects of past trauma associated with negative experiences. Joint research efforts carried out by Dr. John Upledger and biophysicist Dr. Zvi Karni led to the discovery that the body often conserves physical forces rather than dissipates them. It often saves the accompanying emotional energy, unleashed by physiological, psychological, emotional, or spiritual trauma. As the body heals, you can isolate or separate this energy into an "energy cyst." Though a body can initially adapt to the presence of this "energy cyst," it finally weakens or gets tired of hosting it. As a result, symptoms such as pain, dysfunction, or emotional stress may develop.

II. Emotional release techniques - Essentially, an emotional version of acupuncture, save for the fact that we don't use needles. On the contrary, we stimulate certain points on the body's meridians by pressing on them with our fingers. This technique has been used successfully to treat PTSD syndrome in war veterans.

III. Traditional Chinese Acupuncture - My favorite, since it's part of my acupuncture practice, where emotions affect specific organs that project as organic diseases in the body. Rebalancing the organ involved removes the associated symptom.

IV. Applied Kinesiology (Touch for Health) - Touch for Health is a holistic method derived from applied kinesiology clinical practice. It allows activating the patient's resources to recover his health, with straightforward and efficient techniques. Dr. John Thie created it based on the acupuncture meridians and divided into four levels (I through IV) to initiate us into applied kinesiology knowledge. This system emphasizes the start of recovering health, initially reestablishing structural balance since it's not possible to experience optimal health if the body and muscles are unbalanced. This dynamic acknowledges that human beings possess different aspects: physical, biochemical, emotional, intellectual, and spiritual, and that all require balancing.

We Wounded Warriors are like Prisoners Locked Away in the Prison of the Matryoshkas (Russian Dolls)

We must remember that, as in all battles, Warriors' injuries impact the emotional realm as much as the physical. Also, emotional injuries are more severe since the younger recruits have less training and experience. Experiencing the pain and fear associated with his emotional wounds, the Warrior interprets them as caused by being forsaken by his Masters at Arms and fellow unit members in the enemy field. This disconnection imprisons him in solitary confinement, incommunicado in a cell built out of emotional bars by his jailer, the ego.

The Emotional Prisons of the Matryoshkas

Though the Warrior may physically escape and rejoin his unit, these prison experiences are recorded in the past of his subconscious memory, like the Matryoshka dolls encapsulate one within another. These subconscious experiences can only demand your attention by shouting with physical and mental bodily symptoms that seemingly pop out of nowhere.

For the Warriors, they are like experiences recorded in the past that repeat endlessly. These recurrent experiences create his battle-originated schizophrenia and the physical and mental symptoms that affect many Warriors. The only solution for these Warriors are the healing techniques described in the manual and the Warrior of Light's first aid kit (see previous material).

You can use any of the previously described techniques, but I find a method developed by neurolinguistics to be more efficient.

Freeing Our Wounded Warrior with a Reconnection Trip to the Past ("Back to the Future").

This exercise aims to release the wounded Warrior trapped in his past, wholly isolated within his Russian dolls. The woeful part of his imprisonment is that he is permanently stuck in his past, totally disconnected from his future. He lives in a repeating

174

and continuous experience from his past without finding any resolution, good or bad! This incarceration happens as a result of not learning the lesson of love. Because of his spiritual immaturity in this stage of his life, the Warrior cannot decipher the event and only wants to abolish it from his memory. I postulate that the mind's mechanism to minimize these memories of suffering is similar to editing out the difficult parts of our memories as if they were part of a feature film. In our minds, we screen the entire movie and find the unwanted parts. Later, we edit them out.

The film scenes that were left on the cutting room floor get stored in the deepest parts of our subconscious archival vaults, removing them from the short-term memories (RAM) of our mind. This permits the Warrior to continue his trajectory without the painful memories of his past. This censorship of our difficult and shameful experiences begins to subconsciously create emotional jails that trap the Warrior in his past in that traumatic moment in his life, creating a disconnect from the true rough cut of events to the final edited version of memories. Since they don't have a relationship to prior or later events, these edited segments simply form a loop, which is continuously repeated in the subconscious of the person who edited the segment. All this means that the human trapped in that movie segment lives a terrible existence, repeating it continuously.

This part of the Warrior, who feels abandoned by their brother, screams at him and asks his brother to be freed from the jail he created. Being in the subconscious levels of the mind, using its relations with the central nervous system to develop a bombardment of various physical and emotional symptoms as cries for his freedom.

The Warrior that lives in his present and participates in his battles, when he can recall his prison experience, tends to consciously block out his memories, unconsciously weakening his self-esteem in his wounded Warrior of the past. These subconscious prison experiences are at the root of emotional and

176

physical processes undergone by the Warrior, apparently unrelated to his life in the present.

We must first identify the events associated with the battle experience that imprisoned the Warrior. This can be achieved by therapists that help us identify them using the listed techniques (hypnosis, NLP, kinesiology, etc.). But, I believe, this rescue mission must be carried out in secret, self-guided by the Warrior in the present-future, and not by a therapist.

After doing this, we are ready for our secret mission.

The Secret Mission to Free Our Captive Warrior Brother from His Concentration Camp Is The Key To Forgiveness

Preparation

First, you can carry out the Warrior of Light meditation and read his oath.

In a private place whose energy we have already purified following chapter X techniques, we see ourselves seated in a huge and beautiful movie theater, with a screen that projects in 3D. We're playing two parts, first-row spectator and projectionist in the control room. Privacy and monitoring of the projection guarantee the confidentiality and security of the process. If the experience turns too intense, we can shut down the projector and exit the theater.

The Technique

We will recall every detail of the event and project the edited segment, in full color and 3D, how it was, how it begins, its progression, and its outcome. We include all event participants and, at the end of the crisis, of the outcome that imprisons us, we observe ourselves, and note all of the emotions that show up and ask ourselves, "Did that Warrior have the tools or capacity to understand and process the experience? Did he deserve the experience due to his previous immediate actions? The logical reply would be "no."

The spectator Warrior rises motivated by his guilt and shame and attempts a quantum leap to penetrate the image. He rises from his seat and climbs a staircase next to the projection screen. As he pulls back the curtains next to the screen, he can see a door with a sign that says, "The door to the movie of my past." Now motivated by his will to help his brother, he knocks on the door, and when it opens, he is confronted with his past self, who immediately asks, Who are you? Can I help you? The Warrior from the future replies, "I am you, coming from years ahead in the future. I'd like to tell you about how you became imprisoned in this jail because of my irresponsibility, and I'd like to ask for forgiveness. Brother, to free you from this jail, I need you to let me into your time. But first, I would like to thank you and give you a congratulatory hug." His younger brother rebukes him, "Why do you congratulate me?" And his older brother replies, "Because I am alive because you did not take an irreversible decision with your life, and dared to be victorious by exiting your prison."

His older brother enters, hugs him, and asks for forgiveness for having ignored him in his subconscious

179

emotional prison. In the present, the Warrior searches through the entire movie of his life, looking for the segment where he erased the moment from his memory. He then replaces this scene with the original. Once the movie's continuity is restored, the imprisoned Warrior immediately recalls who he is and all of his past. He feels restored, forgiven, and loved. He tells his brother, "Please forgive me for all the symptoms I have caused in your body so that you would become conscious of my suffering and rescue me from this prison." The older brother from the present answers, "Little brother, everything you have done to me, I have deserved, I was a coward and abandoned you in a difficult moment that I should have shared with you." They both embrace and continue on their journeys as Warriors of Light.

If we analyze all the suffering these Warriors experienced and the characters and events external to them that could have caused suffering, we will see that this suffering was not the cause of their imprisonment. It was only a factor and not the cause of the suffering, self-inflicted by the lack of understanding of the lesson of Love hidden in the experience. The very Warriors, separated by their emotional isolation from the event, created the suffering. Because of this, in my opinion, self-forgiveness is the most critical component in physical and mental healing in our lives, not forgiving others that have acted against us because "they know not what they do."

Meditation of The Warrior of Light: The Alchemy of Forgiveness that Transmutes all Metals, or Toxic Emotions, into Golden Love with the Philosopher's Stone that Is the Magical Mirror

This technique uses forgiveness as the alchemy that acts as the philosopher's stone within the Magical Mirror and helps transmute toxic emotions from emotional battle wounds into love and understanding (gold). This technique consists of awakening in the Warrior memories of his origins in the light, so he can recognize them in his mirror-mind and recall the coordinates for returning to his starting point.

The true spiritual alchemy is the transmutation of guilt into co-responsibility and karma into dharma. This represents the ultimate purpose of our learning before we travel back to our real home and frees us, finally, from the suffering created by the ego's illusory individuality.

All of this process is facilitated by the codes, resembling keys obtained by victories in internal and external battles, and which slowly allow the Warrior to recall his lost universal language to decode his luminous DNA from the Akashic Archives. These codes are like keys formed in the sacred geometry that facilitate opening interdimensional doors between destinations.

The Warrior of Light's Final Armistice with the Warrior of Shadows in His Triangular Cosmic Embrace of Knowledge, Understanding, and Love, which Originates the Star of Peace

This process will only be successful if the Warrior of Shadows desists from his toxic lifestyle, modulating his ego with Love and eliminating the use of recreational drugs, junk food, animal foods, irresponsible sexuality, ecological irresponsibility with his planet, economic ambition, social injustice, religious proselytism, politics, and pharmacological toxicity.

Any form of meditation is the most efficient way to reestablish communication with the universal language if combined with the right thoughts and intention, the right words, and the right action. This assures the Warrior that his actions, generated by the law of cause and effect, will lead to dharma, or loving experiences, for himself and others and not karma. The meditation that I recommend for the Warriors of Light is where the Warrior bathes in colorful light, which purifies him with the balm of forgiveness and reconnects him with his Warrior of Light and his Magical Mirror.

Meditation of a Colorful Bath of Light

Seated in a comfortable position with our back straight and our head held up high, let's visualize in our mirror, a source of spiritual strength or energy that makes us feel protected. For example, the figure of the Warrior of Light, or any preferred religious figure, young-looking, smiling, and standing, with open arms and beaming rays of multicolored light from the center of his heart to ours, in which a mirror with a small seed exists.

Let's understand the meaning of the exercise. The Warrior represents the human manifestation of the light, which is the force of love reflected from its Magical Mirror so that we could know the immensity of its creation. The multicolored rays represent the infinite ways in which love may manifest, or reflects, among us. The seed in our heart represents the Warrior of Light's passive form that dwells in the Warrior of Shadows.

As those rays of light fill our heart-mirror, we feel ourselves loved and protected by said love and observe how the small seed starts to open and, in turn, beams the multiple colors of love in all directions.

184

Initially, let's imagine that those colors bathe us in a loving light and penetrate every part of our bodies, especially those where there are some emotional scars, and let's see how these are soothed and healed.

After we are filled with happiness and wellness, we're going to share this with all other Warriors, especially those who have hurt us because they don't know their light.

Visualize multicolored rays beams from our heart-mirror towards all Warriors without distinction, including those who have left this world, and those that, according to us, have brought suffering to our lives. Let's dedicate a few minutes to this action, and then let's rest our mind in silence for a few more minutes. Let's finish by giving thanks for this opportunity. Let's do this exercise every day upon waking and when going to sleep.

Finally, to keep our mind in a peaceful state, let's imagine that our thoughts are like clouds in the sky and that our natural, peaceful state is like the blue color in the sky. Let our thoughts pass like clouds, without following them, focusing on the blue of the sky, our natural state.

The Warrior of Light's Code of Conduct for a Healthy Life

This manual is inspired by the Manual For Healthy Living, written by an anonymous author, and includes some of its content.

Health:

1. Drink lots of water.

2. Eat breakfast like a king, lunch like a prince, and have dinner like a pauper.

3. Eat more foods that grow on trees and plants and less of those processed in factories.

4. Live with the three E's - Energy, Enthusiasm, and Empathy.

5. Set time apart to meditate in silence for at least ten minutes.

6. Waste some time playing a game.

7. Read more and of better quality than you did last year.

8. Sleep at least seven hours a day.

9. Exercise according to your age and fitness at least thirty minutes a day, and smile at everyone you meet.

Personality:

1. Don't compare your life with that of other people, since you will never know how the story ends for each one of you.

2. Don't bother with inevitable events. Focus your mind on the present, on what flows well.

3. Don't overdo it; know your limitations.

187

4. Don't take yourself so seriously! Nobody else does!

5. Don't waste your energy hearing gossip because it will come back to haunt you!

6. It costs nothing to dream: not dreaming costs more!

7. Envy limits us and inhibits, acknowledging our innate creative potential.

8. Don't live in the past, nor make others remember it unless you remember good things.

9. Hate is the poison we brew for others but drink it ourselves!

10. Let's learn to acknowledge and forgive our mistakes to understand those committed by others.

11. Our happiness is our responsibility; don't delegate it to others.

12. Let's understand that life is a constant school of learning by levels, where we must be patient with those in lower levels and admire those in the upper ones.

13. Allow yourself many outbursts of laughter.

14. No one is right all the time, save for the moments that the data has not changed yet.

Social:

1. Keep in touch with your biological and spiritual family.

2. Every day, give a little bit of the best you've got, but don't overdo it!

3. Free yourself from your burdens by forgiving ceaselessly.

4. Set aside some time to gain wisdom from those older than seventy and younger than six.

5. Be a comedian, and make everyone laugh a lot.

189

6. What others think about you is not as important as how you feel about yourself.

7. For others, work is work; for you, work should be a pleasure and a privilege.

Life:

1. Act according to your values, but don't demand that others do the same and avoid frustrations!

2. Don't hoard material things, hoard only updated knowledge, since it does not depreciate.

3. Time is the best medicine if we're patient.

4. The sun always comes up after the storm.

5. No matter how you feel, don't vent your trash on others.

6. Hold on fast to the optimism arising from faith.

7. When you open your eyes at dawn, be thankful for new opportunities to correct your life!

8. Your true self never gives up and is available 24/7. Why don't you use it more often?

And last, but not least:

1. Share this with your friends and enemies.

Exercises

1. Practice the Meditation of the Warrior of Light.

2. Review your conduct throughout the various stages of your life.

CHAPTER IX

THE DEATH OF THE WARRIOR IS A TEMPORARY VOYAGE (ROUND TRIP) TO HIS ANCESTORS' KINGDOM OF VALHALLA: AN OASIS OF REST AND REHABILITATION FOR THE EMOTIONAL WOUNDS FROM HIS BATTLES

Almost at the end of the book, I realized I avoided the most repellent topic for human beings: death. Therefore, as a good Warrior of Light, I decided to face the shadows in my mirror and courageously take up this topic, though apprehensively.

As the birth of the Warrior of Shadows is a creation or illusion of his mirror-mind's shadows, so is the destruction of the material mirage that we call death. To understand this, we must be aware that the

193

Warriors' interdimensional voyages are mental, carried out by their Magical Mirror reflections. The more it distances itself from its source of light, the more the experiences turn denser and more real in his temporal perception until they reach the maximum tridimensional space-time density. Here the Warrior of Light, in his emotional blindness, creates or sees the reflection of his shadow, the Warrior of Shadows, in his mind-mirror.

Upon entering this dimension, all laws and rules of the material realm take effect. This is the realm of contrasts, emotional hues, opposites, the good and the bad, mine and yours, which originates the ego and its need for attachment to that which provides pleasure and detachment from what begets suffering (review chapter I).

When the Warrior's mirror-mind sheds the fictitious vehicle that is his body, it returns to the dimensional realms of the anti-material universe. There, Warriors meet with Masters at Arms that help

194

them understand and heal their emotional wounds as causal experiences for learning new and better tactics for future battles. During this vacation leave, Warriors are reclassified into hierarchies of ranks obtained by their victories and will be assigned more responsibility in their next battlegrounds. We can think about death as expressed in this quote:

Don't look at death as the end of our story, but rather as the beginning of another.

This process shall go on until the Warrior progresses to Master at Arms, which will allow him to influence many groups of Warriors of Shadows in the battles of his earthly experience.

These Masters at Arms, as they help other Warriors find their light once more, keep progressing on their way back, until their light and their shadow intertwine.

They comprehend that it was never necessary to fight for the light since, all along, as in the Yin-Yang symbol, the shadow potentially rests within the light, and their light rests within the shadow. And it is within that balanced union of colors of the light that they resolve their state of battle-originated schizophrenia. That is the birth of the Star of Light, which may manifest all light's qualities in the material worlds, living with its feet firmly grounded, but with its eyes gazing at the heavens.

The Law of Cause and Effect or Law of Love: Free Will and Intention
The Disciplinary Manifestation of Love

From previous chapters, we must recall that the multidimensional holographic matrix interweaves with the matrix of love in a harmonious balance that protects it continuously due to the impersonal law of cause and effect. This law, which is applicable at all dimensional levels of existence, manifests according to the knowledge of the cause and understanding of the effect, activated by the Warrior's intention, and depending on his travel experience.

196

Free will, which also figures from the start with the law of cause and effect, is progressively limited in Warriors' actions as they explore with their mind-mirror the new reflections or shades of light. These start to amplify as more traveler-Warriors classify them as good or bad as per their emotional experiences. As the variability of the experiences increases, so does the difficulty of choosing the right experience.

Due to their light's purity, warriors from higher dimensions can better understand the effects because they possess purer knowledge of the cause. They live in a constant temporal state of the present, including the past (reason) and the future (effect) in continuity. These are the veterans of many battles in all dimensional planes, who have accumulated their experiences and carry them back as souvenirs for their home, the Magical Mirror.

But we must understand that the law's primary purpose is to reestablish balance, altered by the different types of actions, utilizing results that re-balance it to achieve harmony in the matrix. At no moment is the law punitive, but rather corrective and fair in its action, though a Warrior may interpret it as unfair or unpleasant, which he created with his causes.

Intention and Its Relationship with the Law of Cause and Effect

The nature of the intention classifies the manifestation as good (dharma) or bad (karma), depending on how it affects the multidimensional holographic matrix and the Warrior. The intention varies according to the Warrior's trip experience, and we can divide it into two types:

1. Selfish Intention (Warrior of Shadows) – This is the darkest one due to his mirror-mind's clouded vision, created by his ego. It's guided by the effects on "me" and not on "us." It generates karma and results that unbalance the matrix. This intention is the leading cause of the defeated Warriors that live in the shadows and who cannot leave the cycle of birth, old age, and death (Samsara).

198

2. Loving Intention (Warrior of Light) - This one is ruled by the law of love, knowledge of causes, and understanding the effects over the matrix of all Warriors. It generates dharma and results that balance the matrix.

The following quote describes that:

When the Warrior learns to see the universe by reflecting on the Magical Mirror, he only sees the light or love.

And we must recall the importance of how we use our free will, as these quotes indicate:

Every loving intention always matures to yield beneficial effects, but we must be patient because it happens in God's own time and not in ours.

Let us use our free will responsibly since we will have to heed its consequences.

How Free Is Our Free Will?

We must understand that our experience, inheritance, intelligence, congenital disabilities, age, laws, financial condition, and spiritual level influence our capacity to make decisions and that it will change continually as these factors change. This should help us understand that the factors mentioned above limit our mistakes from prior experiences, and we must never blame or judge ourselves for them.

We Cannot Change Past Mistakes without Changing Our Present

Humorously, I offer my patients who feel guilt a trip in a time machine to change their decisions in the past but explain to them that we erase our future by traveling to the past. Therefore, when they return to the very instant in the past without knowing the future outcome, they will repeat the same mistakes. This would imply that if I change my past, I would be a different person in this present! What we experienced, good or bad, resulted from the law of cause and effect and my past intentions, and it was what I needed to learn my lesson during that part of my battle.

Justice-Compassion-Understanding, Injustice-Pity-Dissatisfaction

Warriors of Shadows perceive the apparent discrepancy between good and bad experiences undergone by those with the most limitations as unjust. For example, unjust experiences would be babies' and children's diseases, extreme poverty, etc. They would gaze with disdainful pity at those involved, without realizing that it could happen to them. These Warriors question the nature of the experience by asking why, and by doing so, they cut off their connection to the light source.

Warriors of Light perceive bad experiences as effects that re-balance previous actions or causes and allow the person who caused them to learn and correct them. They feel compassion and empathy for those affected, but not pity. These Warriors ask, "what are these for?" accepting those experiences as lessons of love and not punitive actions.

Homework

Repeat the Meditation of the Warrior of Light

Bonus Questions

1. Differentiate human justice from spiritual justice in the law of cause and effect.

2. Are there punitive effects in the spiritual law of love?

3. Differentiate a compassionate attitude from pity towards other persons.

4. What helps us be compassionate towards others?

CHAPTER X

STEALTHY TACTICS TO WIN THE BATTLE ON THE INTERNAL FRONT: MEDITATION TECHNIQUES

To win the internal battle with our archenemy and supreme commander of the army of shadows, the ego, we must start to learn about his army's forces and future tactics silently, and infiltrate methods and tactics to illuminate the mirror-minds of his Warriors. By using the communications media with a secret coding, the universal archetypes or feelings in their luminous DNA can be awakened, which will lead them to recognize their Warrior of Light in the images of their mirrors (see chapter 6).

The Archetypes or Universal Feelings

These are the knowledge that generates wisdom, the understanding that fosters patience, the empathy that produces compassion, and the love that unites all of them in forgiveness. In turn, these originate a myriad of positive feelings, which help Warriors acknowledge and respect the light in each Warrior, no matter which battle they are in.

Stealth Tactics to Win the Internal Battle

Besides the tactics that we included in the Warrior's First Aid Kit (see chapter 8), we will dedicate this chapter to meditation and its variants as the most silent weapons for this end.

What is meditation?

It complements prayer or verbal communication. Prayer aims our message towards the transcendental, like a message left on an answering machine. Since the signal is limited to our space-time tridimensional dimension, we will never be sure if it was received without a receipt confirmation. We must try to reestablish our communication with our Warrior of Light in our Magical Mirror, using the archetypal and luminous meditation language. Besides the codes obtained by our victories in the external battles, meditation is another form of receiving more codes and tactics that will back us up in our battlefronts.

With meditation, we shall begin our return journey to our origins and realize our true nature. By this means, we shall find the answer to the three existential questions that we bear for a long time:

Who am I? Where do I come from? Where am I going?

Meditation - Definition

Meditation is a self-directed technique whereby we focus our mental processes, internally or externally, to establish physical and mental relaxation that calms down all thought activity. This state fosters pleasant, harmonious, and precise physiological effects in the body.

There are multiple variations on the basic technique, but they all target the same goal and results. The ultimate aim is to completely stop the constant mental chatter, creating silent spaces inside us that correspond to the black holes, or the Yin phase, of the material universe. Those quiet spaces are like the interdimensional gaps between the visible (material) universe and the transcendental or anti-material universe.

We must recall that our emotional smudges could distort how we process and remember the experience upon seeing our image in our mirror-mind. This must instill in us caution in acknowledging that other Warriors could differ from our way of interpreting them and not make them into religions or separatist sectarian philosophies.

In time, the universal feelings of the transcendent Magical Mirror will begin to manifest in us, and we will also start to acknowledge them in the other Warriors.

Documented Benefits of Meditation

From Dr. Henry Benson's "The Relaxation Response":

206

1. An increase in the generation of alpha brain waves

2. A decrease in heart rate

3. A reduction in basal oxygen consumption

4. An increase in electro-cutaneous resistance

5. A decrease in lactic acid levels in muscles

Other Documented Benefits

1. A decrease in nerve conductivity

2. A drop in blood pressure

3. It decreases bronchial asthma episodes

4. It calms insomnia

5. It reduces anxiety and the need for drugs

Meditation: Preparation and Prerequisites

1. The proper attitude

2. The proper place

3. The proper time

4. The proper technique(s)

The Proper Attitude

This must be based on the interdependence with other living beings and must show:

1. Wisdom - knowledge, and understanding

2. Humility

3. Creative loving and unselfish intention

4. Respect - all Warriors have their potential light

5. Patience - without temporal demands or expectations, each Warrior progresses at his pace

These are the attributes intrinsic to the Warrior of Light

The Proper Place

It must have the characteristics that foster the appropriate calmness in body and mind.

1. Physical safety and privacy

2. Pleasant temperature

3. Pollution-free atmosphere and air

4. Noise-free

5. Open natural spaces - mountains, near lakes, seas, and forests

It's evident that, in our modern lives, we can't easily access places with all of the previous characteristics, but we can set a private area in our home and give it our personal touch with most of them.

The Proper Time

The usual recommendation is early in the morning when the mind and body are more rested, but it's okay to do it at night for those who feel better at that time. Initially, we must begin with short periods of five to ten minutes, or for the time that we can manage without the body and mind making a fuss. You'll see that, with more experience, meditating for half an hour becomes easy. The ideal frequency would be daily to get better results.

The Proper Technique - Posture

According to all Oriental traditions, body and mind-mirror are interrelated through an endless web of energy channels, concentrated in some areas of the body as energy centers, or chakras. This energy network must be flowing harmoniously for our body to work adequately, and for the mind and body to communicate effectively. The physical body's correct posture is essential for proper circulation.

Though there are many variants, today we shall discuss the seven points of posture recommended by the Buddha Vairocana.

1. Cross the legs in a half-lotus or full lotus.

2. Place the hands on your lap, fingers interlocked, right hand over the left hand with the thumbs slightly touching. An alternative is to place the palms of the hands on your knees.

3. The spinal column must be perfectly vertical.

4. The elbows should not touch the sides of the body. To achieve this effect, we must light the shoulders slightly.

5. The head is slightly bowed forward, but the neck aligns with the spinal column.

6. As for the mouth, the jaw is relaxed and slightly open, the tongue contacts the palate's roof.

7. The eyes are kept naturally, partially open, focusing on the nose or 30 degrees to the front or towards the floor. If they close naturally, it's all right, as long as we don't squint.

Modification of the Sitting Posture

For older adults or those with flexibility problems or otherwise disabled they may meditate sitting down as long as they observe the previous requirements, particularly regarding the back. They must not lean on the chair backrest (see image).

The Technique - Summary

Preparation:

1. Body relaxation (appropriate position and attitude, slight stretching, visualization of a pleasant moment)

2. Creating the mental space (developing the feeling of protection with a circle of Love)

3. Concentration - focusing our mind (Shamata)

4. Freeing the mind and allowing it to fuse with its origins (silence, space, emptiness) (Vipassana)

5. Reintegration to our material reality

6. Merit dedication (giving thanks and sharing)

The Purification of Our Spaces, Sharing Them with Love and Respect

Respect for interdimensional spaces with all visible and invisible beings in creation is the most efficient way to purify them.

Prayer to Purify Spaces Wherever We Are

I ask permission to share this space,

With all beings of the visible and invisible worlds which live here.

And I humbly request that we harmonize all of our energies,

For the benefit of all those that live here and those who are visiting. Thanks.

The Two Tibetan Buddhist Meditation Techniques: Shamata and Vipassana

Shamata (concentration)

At first, the mind behaves like a wild monkey that jumps ceaselessly from branch to branch. The most efficient way to calm the mind is to focus it on external or internal objects.

214

External Shamata

In this technique, we focus our attention on objects with a pleasant meaning, such as:

1. Sacred or religious objects.
2. A lighted candle

Internal Shamata

In this technique, our concentration focus is on our breathing.

When we observe it, we must make sure we do not force it, that when we inhale, we allow the abdomen to expand to allow maximum airflow to our lungs.

Exhalation usually should be considered to take longer than inhalation (twice as long).

In this technique, the intention or effort is to calm down the mind, and we must practice it until we feel comfortable, for periods of at least fifteen minutes.

After mastering this technique, we can go on to Vipassana, where we make no effort. It helps to focus on the expiratory and inspiratory phases of breathing.

Vipassana (Effortless Meditation)

When we have already learned to calm down or focus the mind with this technique, we begin to observe it and let it loose without restricting it. The goal is to observe its nature of unceasing activity, entirely independent of the observer. We must visualize thoughts as clouds drifting in the sky, but they are not the sky. Our true transcendental mind, the Magical Mirror, corresponds to a clear sky, and if we focus on the clouds, we will not see the sky.

Many positive, negative, calming, or exciting thoughts will come, but we must let all of them go by without judging them as good or bad.

When we discover ourselves following each thought anew, then we must refocus our mind on breathing until it calms down, then let go again.

216

Measures to Support Meditation

During the initial stages, some people will need external aids to relax their minds, such as:

1. Incense

2. Music - mantras

3. Altars and religious figures

4. Darkness

Each person will do that which is more comfortable for him or her.

Meditation Complementary Techniques

1. Visualization

2. Analytical contemplation

3. Mindfulness in action - awareness

Visualization

1. It is based on the concept that we, sharing a heritage where this universe originates, can be

co-creators of our future reality by visualizing it in our mirror-mind image.

2. The connection between past, present, and future - we can break the time barrier and create all three periods during the visualization. (See the meditation-visualization of the Warrior of Light in chapter 8.)

3. This technique has been part of the training of great athletes and musical artists in our world.

4. We could compare it to creating a tridimensional painting or movie, where we would appear as real as we look in our daily lives.

5. It's a kind of imaginary creation in our mirror-mind, which we release through the spaces between the dimensions, making it easy for us to manifest that visualized reality in our material world.

Analytical Contemplation

1. It is the method used by many Oriental schools to analytically understand, within the parameters of logic and reason, the reasons behind our universe's structure and origin. It's a method that tries to integrate the material world with the spiritual world using reason.

2. This is the type of contemplation that gave rise to all of the different Oriental philosophies.

Mindfulness In Action - Awareness

1. It is based on the capacity to carry the meditative state's mental awareness over to everyday activities in our lives.

2. It initially depends on observing ourselves or paying more attention to our daily actions and intentions and their effects on others.

3. It's a state of readiness, similar to observing our mind during a sitting meditation where we watch it without judging, but where we remain aware of

our actions' motivations and outcomes upon others.

4. This allows us to avoid inappropriate actions and not repeat them.

5. In time, our actions will be more spontaneous and natural, without the need to control our minds.

Self-Esteem and Guilt

1. One of the many effects of meditation upon the mind is the capacity to improve our self-esteem and soothe our sense of guilt gradually.

2. Depending on our experience during the battles, and on the purity of the images visualized in our mirror-minds, we will all have fears, phobias, and guilt, like emotional battlefield scars.

3. Meditation allows us to understand the truth: We all originate in the luminous world of the Magical Mirror.

4. We all possess the light or the potential to manifest the attributes of this energy. In time, meditation will help us acknowledge it in ourselves and other people and manifest it in our lives.

5. If we review the material covered, we'll see that these shadows were created in our mirror-minds by the distortions in the mirror, created in turn by our emotions.

6. We must realize that due to our matrix of light's holographic link, we are all interdependent, and we must share the merit of both the good and the bad things we've done. We're co-responsible for our mistakes, but not guilty of them.

7. Not knowing that we possess these luminous attributes gives rise to selfish actions, which may create suffering for ourselves and others. This phrase from another one of my books clarifies this concept: There are no bad Warriors. There

are only those who don't yet know they are good.

Homework

1. Put together a session of various practices of the techniques previously described.

Bonus Questions

1. The only inconvenience with this technique is that we can't tell when it will become real. Why? Hint: check the types of intentions and the law of cause and effect.

CHAPTER XI

THE ALCHEMICAL MARRIAGE OF LIGHT AND SHADOW GIVES BIRTH TO THE STAR OF PEACE, WHICH, HAVING ITS FEET ON THE GROUND AND ITS GAZE ON THE HEAVENS, CAN ONLY SEE LOVE IN CREATION

As Above, So Below: The Light and Its Shadow Acknowledge Their Shared Origin: Love

Reaching the end of this journey guided by the light's intention, the Warriors who have been successful in each of their battlefields find the beauty hidden in its counterpart's image reflected in their Magical Mirror. This final battle precipitates the immediate reconnection between the two Warriors from opposing sides, who had set out together without recognizing each other since the beginning of their journey. Hence the phrase, The Warrior of Light is always accompanied by his shadow since, without it, he could never remember his light.

This realization generates the final armistice of this loving struggle, which only wanted to allow the colors of light that each one had, but hadn't experienced, to come out. This armistice manifests in an embrace full of knowledge, understanding, love, and compassion, where the Star of Peace is born, which encompasses all wisdom obtained during its journey through the dual experiences of the jousting Warriors.

That Star of Peace shall be the GrandMaster at Arms who shall bring love epidemics to all the battlefields it visits with his contagious loving nature. For this marvelous union between the dimensional planes of light and shadow to happen, there needs to be reestablishing communications between all levels, retrieving the universal language that bonded them together in the journey's first stages.

224

The Reestablishment of the Universal Language (review Chapter 6)

This quote could summarize the meaning of the universal language: The key that translates this language into our dialect is stored within the luminous DNA, and only veteran Warriors, who have triumphed both in their internal and external battles, can open or decode the supply lines, as they clean up the distortions reflected by their mirrors. And we must remember this other one: The universal language is written in the alphabet of love.

This language slowly "downloads" or decodes from our luminous DNA, with the codes we received through any of these three ways:

1. The Warrior's victories in his internal battlefield (chapter 4)

2. The Warrior's victories in his external battlefield (chapter 5)

3. Meditation techniques

Through those "downloads," universal feelings (see chapter 10) start blooming in the Warriors' mirror-mind, allowing them to reflect its light in all of their battles. They finally achieve the final armistice and the union of the two Warriors in the Grand Master at Arms, the Star of Peace, discussed at the beginning of the chapter.

Before the Warrior's light and shadow can meld into their alchemical offspring, the Star of Peace, the Warrior of Light must acknowledge the light in his enemy, and the Warrior of Shadows must recognize his hidden light. The latter can only happen when the Warrior of Shadows deserts his side and joins the Warrior of Light's team, where he will retrain to condition his Warrior body and join the battle against the Warriors of Shadows. It's at this stage when, using the medals accrued during his internal and external battles and the meditation techniques, he begins to receive the codes from his luminous DNA to transform his biological DNA.

Reprogramming Our Biological DNA; The Last Initiation and Purification Ritual before Consummating the Alchemical Marriage between the Light and Its Shadow

That stage of advancement in his battles starts with the transformation happening in the biological-material DNA due to the influence of the reconnection with its sibling, the luminous DNA, and the reprogramming that began with the codes received from the universal language of love.

The Epigenetic Purification of our Biological Body Takes Place by Correcting the Toxic Lifestyles that Don't Allow Us to Acknowledge Our Light

To purify the toxicity created in our mirror-mind and our biological DNA by the forces of shadows, we must understand its methods.

Methods Used by the Forces of Shadows to Obscure the Brightness of Our Mirror-Mind

The forces of shadows are fictitious creations of our clouding or incapacity to see the true light. Due to the emotional distortions created in our mind-mirror, the only way they can survive is using the ego's favorite weapons to prevent us from viewing the mirror's true image: our light.

Weapons Used by the Ego to Imprison Us in Its Shadows

Our fictitious archenemy, the ego, is an expert in using emotions effectively to generate an extensive arsenal of weaponry, using them to keep the Warrior trapped in the constant cycle of birth, illness, old age, and death. Some of these weapons are selfishness, individualism, ambition, attachment, fear, envy, anger, frustration, arrogance, emotional codependency, corrupt politics, toxic pharmacology, religious sectarianism, diseases, lust, and sexual oppression, social and racial oppression, etc.

The ego's primary goal is to keep altering and distorting our biological DNA's original purity, which at the beginning of creation, reflected the attributes of the luminous DNA better. Since these alterations are influenced by inheritance from ancestors and the fathers' sins, in the Biblical sense, as well as by lifestyles in future generations, this archenemy controls the material realm of shadows to promote lifestyles that foster its goal.

The Epigenetic Influences Used by the Forces of Shadows, which Are Harmful Towards Biological DNA

Chemical Contamination

Mass manufacture, preservation, canning, refrigeration, and commercial agriculture have contaminated the majority of our foodstuffs and bodies of water with an extensive range of chemical compounds of variable toxicity, which alters the quality of the human genome.

Air Pollution

All of the industrial processes, the agricultural ones, and emissions from burning oil and its byproducts, besides causing direct effects in our bodies, also have indirect effects due to the atmospheric changes created.

Electromagnetic Contamination

With the unchecked development of communications media and electronic equipment technology, a toxic bath covers our planet. Due to its slow and progressive effects, it is challenging to document scientifically. Science links an increase in brain tumors, learning problems, abortions, workers' productivity, and Alzheimer's disease. The distressing thing is that the industry can modify equipment to decrease these effects, but governments do not force them to comply.

Pharmacological Contamination

The astronomical development of modern medicine as an industry with a profit motive and not as a human right, and the philosophy of prioritizing the treatment of symptoms over seeking disease causes has triggered very effective drugs with limited specificity. This implies that many drugs, though very useful in lessening symptoms, produce other symptoms or side effects in other body areas that could often be very harmful. Many drugs induce genetic defects in pregnancies, and it wouldn't be unheard of that they could do the same in bodies at different stages of life.

Mental and Emotional Contamination or Programming

One of the most controversial topics discussed by professionals in every educational field is the influence of mass media on personality and lifestyles during different human development stages. Our children and grandchildren are continually bombarded by effective subliminal messages through advertising on TV and on the Internet.

For example, modern superheroes use more violence than their enemies, and, ironically, many of them are mutants! Recently these mass media have become agents of persecution and harassment of every sort, and our privacy is not assured when using them. It's worth asking, what will be the impact on family values for our children by this invasion of aggressive information?

The Detox Program for Our Biological DNA

Physical-Biological Detox

We could condense this detox's goal as lessening the exposure to all industrial and agricultural products that have been processed and contaminated in any way. The ideal thing is to produce or raise our products, but since this is not easy in the major cities, we have to settle for buying quality organic products. The smartest way to increase and decrease their cost is to stop buying contaminated and processed products.

We should assure our water quality by filtering it

with effective methods, which ensure removing the most harmful toxic products. I do not recommend using bottled water due to the chemical contamination that some plastic containers may cause.

Horizontal Genetic Transfer (see Glossary)

It's a genetic modification process, also known as lateral gene transfer (LGT), by which an organism transfers genetic material to another cell that is not a descendant. This aspect of genome alteration is essential because we are continually receiving portions of animal and human DNA in meat and its byproducts, in some drugs and vaccines! Examples of this are recombinant DNA and chimeric DNA (see glossary) used to manufacture some medications.

The potential residual effects in our human DNA from the scientific standpoint are not apparent yet. Knowing industrial ethics as per prior experience, this could cause us to lose some sleep!

Though Hippocrates stated, "Let your food be

233

your medicine, and let your medicine be your food," it would seem that industry misread it: "Let your food be your poison." It's important to note that though modern physicians take the Hippocratic oath, they break it

immediately by denying any therapeutic effect in the quality of our nutrition and supplements!

How Can We Make our Food Be our Medicine?

Life is an ongoing inflammatory process that ages our tissues and drains the battery of our Energizer bunny, which stops moving upon death.

Why see life as an inflammatory process? Let's see the definition of inflammation. Inflammation is a set of reactions generated by the body in response to aggression. This attack may originate externally, like an injury, infection, trauma, or it can come from inside the body, as in autoimmune diseases.

But any process that results from the body's exposure to an agent that it does not recognize as its own will trigger the inflammatory process. That agent may be a mental perception of danger, as happens in the activation of the alarm and protection process that prepares us to fight or flee from potential danger. That process is so inflammatory that it can be chemically

measured by the hormones it segregates, and is what stresses our lives and could result in physical illnesses.

An allergen in the air inflames our respiratory tract and keeps filling the offices - and pockets - of many specialists. Digestive intolerance to certain nutrients, like dairy products and gluten in cereals, produces severe inflammatory effects.

Where Does Intolerance and Allergies to So Many Foods Come From?

To understand this process, we would have to know how industrialization gradually affected agricultural production and how it affected the body. For example, genetic strains of the original grains changed genetically, as they adapted to the places where they grew and to cultivation methods. Farmers favored larger, more productive, and climate-resistant

235

strains and encouraged their planting. These genetic adaptations could lead the body not to recognize them as the original crop, creating an allergic inflammatory reaction. If we consider the amount of new transgenic forms for agricultural products, it wouldn't be surprising to find atypical physical responses.

What foods make up the top seven in the inflammatory list?

1. Alcohol

2. Refined sugar

3. Gluten (refined flours of some cereals)

4. Meats

5. Dairy products

6. Junk, processed, and canned food

7. Trans fats

The Diet Controversy, and My Prejudice in this Matter

If we adhere to the Warrior's manual and its tactics to recodify our biological DNA, we're forced to choose food that is:

1. The least processed or refined

2. The least transgenic

3. The freshest

4. The ones that most resemble their original form

5. The lowest in gluten

6. Without any dairy content

7. Without any animal product or byproduct content

8. Derived from products in season

9. The lowest in refined sugar

10. The lowest in total calories (partial fasts)

The only scientific findings acknowledged as promoting longevity and quality of life were low-calorie, low refined sugar diets!

Influence Upon Eating Styles

1. Fasting - Recent studies of ethnic groups who use intermittent fasting by limiting the amount and frequency of food intake have shown beneficial effects regarding longevity and health. I recommend reading up a bit on the topic and taking advantage of this knowledge for your health. (Read the book on fasting listed in the bibliography.)

2. Mono-diet - Fasting variant based on not mixing different foods in the same meal to facilitate digestion and lower inflammation. This contradicts the nutritional theory that posits mixing many colors on your plate, like an Impressionist painting! It's preferable to distribute the colors in different meals.

3. Do not mix many liquids with your meals or drink them cold, as they decrease the proper absorption of nutrients.

4. Sprouted or raw foods - I don't think this works for every occasion, but it can be combined with traditional vegan diets and could be one more way to detox a sick body.

So my recommendation to belong to the Warriors of Light unit tends towards a vegan diet, or modified vegan, according to each body's needs. We don't want any animal DNA nor transgenic products in our food.

A recap

Dear readers, I have thoroughly enjoyed being a tour guide proud of his region, having escorted you through the Warrior of Light's different adventures. I hope I have helped you find your return coordinates so your time machine can take you home in the deepest part of the Magical Mirror, our creator. Remember to be patient, as the following quotes, learned from my

Master at Arms, say:

Though all paths lead you to Heaven, they don't all get you there simultaneously.

The weapons of the true Warrior of Light are compassion and the patience to wait for the other person to learn what he has already learned.

Discovering our Mission or Purpose in Life - A Summary of What We Have Learned so Far, and a Prelude of What We Will Study Next

The most important thing for those experimenting with the infinite and multidimensional trip of knowledge and understanding is discovering their mission within the cosmic one. They must progressively increase their activity as their free will becomes more inclusive and open to different possibilities.

We could compare this to the melodic impact of the music created by the instrument used by a musician playing his or her composition, within a harmonious symphony directed by an experimented director.

Even though the musical impact of the musician's actions may be incredible, it will never compare to the sensation of belonging to a grand symphony. All the musicians are equally crucial for a director who only aspires to merge all the instruments harmoniously. Just like our cosmic experience could be represented by the person who learns to create music in every musical instrument, and then joins other musicians and collaborates in more inclusive creations. This facilitates cosmic symphonies that will become progressively more complicated by accumulating knowledge from individual instrumental experiences.

Similarly, the individual voyage's initial experience progresses to a planetary journey, then to a solar, galactic, universal, and cosmic journey.

This is the inexorable infinite cycle that combines the experience of evolving, learning, ascending, or teaching, with the learning from the other travelers who follow us in our cosmic path.

The cycle finally ends in the cosmic conscience's real individuality, where new and infinite universal creations are born and discovered throughout our continuous astral travels.

Therefore, we should understand the importance of each of our lives' experiences, which, directed by the interdependent intention of love's strength and pain's suffering, always result in the acquisition of knowledge through understanding and compassion.

This is the secret of the true spiritual alchemy that transforms each experience in knowledge. Forgiveness is the philosopher's stone, or catalyst, that allows the understanding that accelerates the transmutation.

Bonus Questions

1. How does the Warriors' alchemical marriage influence the reconciliation of the luminous and biological DNAs?

2. Why is the universal voyage a round trip?

3. Why don't all Warrior-voyagers return at the same time?

4. Why is forgiveness the healing balm and decoding key for the spiritual DNA?

5. What can you infer will happen when all Warriors have returned?

CHAPTER XIII

FINAL EXAM FOR THE WARRIORS OF LIGHT

Instructions: Choose the best answer among the options

1. What is antimatter?

   a) That which occupies the greater part of our universe (72%)

   b) What science says gave rise to matter

   c) A new socialist party that opposes unchecked consumerism

   d) What ghosts are made of

2. We can state the following about our DNA:

   a) It came from monkeys

245

b) It has in its files the Warrior's biological history as well as his spiritual one

c) 100% is used for its hereditary encoding function

d) All of the above

3.   Junk DNA is:

a) The dumping site for all of our mutations

b) The one occupying 3-5% of the total

c) The control panel that encodes for the human genome

d) All of the above

4.   The Akashic Registry:

a) Is where all birth certificates are filed in India

b) They are the virtual archives with the records of all of the Warriors' experiences during their journeys

c) It's the book that stores all of our karma

d) B and C

5. Epigenetics is:

a) A new branch of biology

b) What explains how environmental influences facilitate or inhibit hereditary genetic tendencies

c) Where junk DNA plays a vital role

d) All of the above

6. Regarding free will, we might say that:

a) It's the same for every Warrior

b) Makes you responsible for the effects of your actions

c) Each Warriors' individual experience affects his "freedom" to act

d) B and C

7. The Magical Mirror is:

a) Our time machine or primordial mind

b) That which gives rise to the transcendental mind and the relative mind

c) That which potentially contains all of the creative processes of the universe

d) All of the above

8. The ego is:

a) Our realistic mirror

b) Our fictitious archenemy or dragon created by our emotions

c) He who loves individualism and competition

d) All of the above

9. Quantum entanglement:

a) Proves the universe's holographic continuity

b) Is described in the phrase, "All for one and one for all."

c) Is how protons and electrons reproduce

d) A and B

10. The only thing all Warriors agree on is that:

a) They prefer to be vegans

b) They like their reflection in their mirror-mind

c) They want to be happy

d) All of the above

11. Chimeric DNA is:

a) When genetic material from two species
   mixes randomly in genetic experiments

b) When part of the genetic material of one
   species incorporates into another in an
   experiment

c) The mutation that originates the super
   mutants from the TV series

d) None of the above

12. Battle-originated schizophrenia is:

a) The state of confusion and suffering that rules
   the battlefield relationship between the
   Warrior of Light with his shadow, the Warrior
   of Shadows

b) A state where no one knows who the enemy is, which army to battle with, and what tactics will be best for victory

c) Something that can lead the Warrior to a severe mental imbalance

d) All of the above

13. The true origin of suffering is:

a) Extreme capitalism and humanity's social and economic inequality

b) Corruption in governments

c) The void that originates within us (battle-originated schizophrenia) when we disconnect from our origins, the Magical Mirror

d) All of the above

14. Which of the following is the most useful attribute to achieve victory on the battlefield?

a) Intelligence

b) Persistence

c) Prayer

d) Patience or compassion

15. The Warrior's tactics to decode his lost universal language are:

a) Victories in his external and internal fronts

b) Meditation

c) Healing the wound of the imprisoned Warriors of Shadows with forgiveness and compassion

d) All of the above

16. Meditation is:

a) A "wireless" communication technique in a format similar to our original universal language

b) It was one of the tactics that our Masters at Arms taught us

c) It helps us decode our supply lines in the battle with our light source, the Magical Mirror

d) All of the above

17. Compassion is:

a) When our heart "breaks" and we get mad at the injustices that man does to other men

b) When we allow others to mistreat us, even though inside we are furious

c) When we learn to see all Warriors in the reflection of our Magical Mirror with the same love

d) All of the above

18. The most efficient tactic to escape from our archenemy ego's prison is forgiveness:

a) Arising from understanding our responsibility based on ignorance

b) Because both the ego and its prison were an illusory creation generated by our negative emotions

c) Because it not only frees us from our prison bars but also makes the jailer disappear

d) All of the above

19. Guilt:

a) Is the ego's favorite weapon to trap the Warrior of Light in its shadows

b) Is based on the lie that, in every universal experience of the Warrior, only one person is guilty of the effect

c) Turns into co-responsibility within the holographic vision of a universe quantum entangled by love

d) All of the above

20. The goals given to the Warrior of Light by his Magical Mirror when setting out were:

    a) To begin an exploratory trip to the universe, which starts at the love that seeks to meet its creation and understand its purpose

    b) To be guided by solidarity, empathy, compassion, and patience during his voyage

    c) To rescue most of the Warriors of Light from the prisons where the ego had locked them up using the previous techniques

    d) All of the above

21. The outer battlefront flanks are:

    a) Family, academic, religious, work-related

    b) Frontal, right, left

    c) Emotional, mental, spiritual, military

d) None of the above

22. Spiritual blindness is:

a) The distortion created in the Mirror by the emotional scars of his battles

b) The visual distortion created by his weapons' gunpowder wounds

c) The visual distortion created by shrapnel explosions

d) None of the above

23. In the allegorical comparison of the Hansel and Gretel fairy tale, emotions were represented by:

a) The breadcrumbs

b) The candies

c) The birds

d) The witch

24. Why can the Warriors of Shadows never be happy?

a) Because all of the mirror's experiences change continually

b) Due to selective attachment to certain pleasant experiences

c) Due to individualism and envy, and differences in the Warriors' capacities, experiences, medals, and rank

d) All of the above

25. What did the tower of Babel represent?

a) The location of the high command of the Warriors of Shadows

b) The attempt to return to the starting point, which some Warriors tried to do at the beginning without finishing their mission

c) The capacity to use his universal language to help himself return home

d) B and C

26. The differences between the rules of engagement in both battlefronts are:

a) In the internal front, the Warrior of Light is an active participant

b) In the external front, the Warrior of Light only participates as an adviser to the Warriors of Shadows

c) The Warrior of Light take an active part in both

d) A and B

27. The inner battle is the most dangerous one for the Warrior because:

a) The internal Warrior of Shadows uses guerrilla, espionage and infiltration tactics that subtly weaken our strengths

b) Signs of the attacks manifest themselves as symptoms both physical and mental, in very advanced epidemic forms (depression, anxiety, phobias, insomnia, cancer, alterations to cognitive capacity, etc.)

c) It can be backed simultaneously by the Warriors in the external battle.

d) All of the above

28. Intention and its effect upon the law of cause and effect:

a) The loving, interdependent intention generates effects that balance all of the holographic matrix (dharma)

b) The individual, independent, selfish intention produces effects that unbalance the matrix (karma)

c) It does not have a punitive effect; it only wants to understand its effect on the matrix

d) All of the above

29. The Biblical quote, "Punishing the children for the Sin of the parents to the third and fourth generation" (Numbers 14:18), proves:

a) The influence of epigenetics upon inheritance

b) How diseases can be inherited

c) That changing lifestyles cannot correct Sin

d) A and B

30. To be effective, forgiveness as the universal healing balm has to:

a) Be based on the understanding and compassion acquired from our success in battle

b) Be based upon selfishness that rejects the adverse effects of karma

c) Be based on practices undertaken by others on our behalf to cancel karma

d) None of the above

EPILOGUE

THE STORY BEHIND MY SCHOOL OF LIFE BOOK TRILOGY

To understand how my book trilogy takes shape, we must first understand how the creative process arises historically, in the natural sciences and the humanities. When we review the history of the significant advances in art and the natural sciences, we can observe a trend whereby new ideas appear in sets, nearly simultaneously, in geographically distant places and in eras where today's mass media interconnectivity was lacking. Because of these common disagreements over who "created" the idea, the laws still divide the global community into intransigent camps, centuries after the event.

Even in modern times, we can see this phenomenon at the Nobel Prize science award ceremony. During my experimental research year, the same thing happened to me. Every time I came up with a hypothesis, other academic centers with more extensive financial resources published them, thought up by others. This phenomenon was repeated during my pediatric surgery educational experience when I designed a new surgical procedure for Congenital Megacolon disease. Before I had the chance to publish my findings, I found out that a Mexican surgeon had already published it three months before! I felt like the silver medalist who came in second by a few milliseconds at the Olympics, and nobody remembers him.

Though a significant portion of discoveries manifests after exhaustive efforts and analysis, often great scientific minds concede that their idea was born from apparent serendipity (see glossary), or pure intuition or "chance." An example of serendipity in science: The discovery of penicillin. In 1922, when

Alexander Fleming analyzed a bacterial culture, a Petri dish became contaminated with a fungus. He would later discover that the bacteria would not grow around the fungus and imagined that something there was killing them. Though he was not able to isolate it, the episode gave rise to the discovery of penicillin.

Another example was when chemist Friedrich Kekulé had been trying to discover benzene's elusive structure for a long time. Quite simply, a six-carbon structure with the chemical properties of the benzene molecule was unknown. As he told it in his memoirs, he fell asleep one afternoon while returning home on the bus. He started dreaming about atoms that danced and collided among themselves. Several atoms united, forming a snake shaped like a letter "s". Suddenly, the snake bit its tail, and Kekulé woke up. No one had thought until that moment that benzene might be a cyclic compound.

Bob Samples, in his book The Metaphoric Mind: A Celebration Of Creative Consciousness, said he interpreted Albert Einstein's work when he wrote, "The intuitive mind is a sacred gift, and the rational mind is a faithful servant. We have created a society that honors the servant and has forgotten the gift." This quote reflects the importance of the balance between the rational mind and its creative counterpart. This reflection is so on point that it is incorrectly attributed to Einstein himself.

Einstein recognized serendipity as a quality in some of his findings, which was the reason for his propensity to stimulate creativity in the school system. The following quote indicates he suggests challenging all previously accepted knowledge since he believed that real knowledge was an infinitely changing process.

"It is the supreme art of the teacher to awaken joy in creative expression and knowledge." Albert Einstein

Finally, an unknown author penned a rather accurate observation, which I think complements this section of my book very nicely: "The difference

266

between the world's most knowledgeable person and the most ignorant is completely insignificant when you consider what neither knows."

Is Serendipity Only a Matter of Luck, or Coincidences?

To Einstein, as well as Plato (see archetypes in the glossary) and the Buddha, all knowledge existed in a dormant state (see the primordial mind in the glossary) waiting for the mind to discover it, with the appropriate key to unlock its "mysteries." Fortuitous coincidences did not exist for Einstein nor the Buddha, but rather an ignorance of the cause that precipitated the observed effect. Thus, if we persevere and are patient, we will always find the reason for the "coincidence." These following quotes support this discussion.

"The most beautiful experience we can have is the mysterious. It is the source of all true art and all science." Albert Einstein

"Free from desire, you realize the mystery. Caught in desire, you see only the manifestations. Both arise from the same source. This source is called darkness, the portal towards all the marvels." Lao-Tzu

Therefore, the serendipity that leads to a creative process favors the quality and broadness of knowledge, the researcher's flexible attitude of not hanging onto previously established concepts, and being mindful of these seemingly coincidental changes without discarding them before performing a rational analysis of their prior knowledge. The following famous quotes support my comment.

"In the fields of observation, chance favors the prepared mind." Louis Pasteur

"The seeds of great discoveries always surround us, but they only germinate in our minds if the soil is fertile enough to receive them." Joseph Henry, famous North American physicist

When reviewing the previous material, it would seem that intuition is a cognitive process that does not occur within the traditional rational process associated with the left hemisphere, and which is associated more with the creative process linked to the brain's right hemisphere. It would equally seem that activating the cognitive processes related to the right hemisphere fosters this process. In the future, perhaps the school system will learn to develop this attribute in our students.

The Strange Tale of my Books: My Right Brain Requests Equal Time

To understand the unusual circumstances of the books' creation, you must know that my experience as a writer began relatively late in my professional life, at age 70, when most of those who belong to this group are seeking to hang up their gloves, not seeking opponents to try them out. My books' origins could be due to an awakening of the possible attributes in my right brain, requesting equal time from the left one, which manifested itself in a feeling of discontent and unhappiness that nothing in my professional or personal life could dissipate.

This contentious battle between my two hemispheres was exacerbated by my meditative experience during my years practicing Tibetan Buddhism, which, for the first time, channeled my mental focus into introspection. During this period, I learned to know myself, as I wanted to be and not as I had allowed others to tell me I was. Under the thoughtful wisdom of my Master's mirror, I learned to recognize the immensity of the loving attributes that existed hidden in my being, which I had unsuccessfully sought so much in my outside world. Under the persistent requests of my right brain, I made the "illogical" decision of retiring from my surgical practice and dedicating myself to the study of traditional Chinese medical acupuncture and the new, unsure pathways of natural and holistic medicine.

From that moment on, my right brain beat up my left one, and it hasn't let go of my thoughts' cognitive process. Starting then, an indescribable feeling of joy and satisfaction filled my life with the same or an even better sensation than what I obtained with my achievements as a surgeon. I no longer was the same being, and my family, friends, and patients very gratefully observed it. I finally understood the many interpretations of sensitive friends and astrological readings that suggested that I had been inhibiting a significant intuitive potential. My capacity to understand the root of my patients' ailments made it easier for me to help them seek their recovery, as I had found mine.

Approximately ten years ago, during the initial stage of this process, I started hearing an inner voice that pressured me to write a book, but my left brain avoided it and laughed at it. After all, what experience did I have! Finally, on the weekend after a spiritual retreat, I wrote a poem entitled "Soledad" (Loneliness) almost instantly, which eventually was the inspiration for my first book. On another occasion, I wrote a book in a single day, which I called "El libro que aún no tiene título" (The Book Which Has No Title Yet), and which I believed to be a work of art. Under the spell of my innocent literary illusion, I quickly shared my "gem" with my best friends and family, and, to my chagrin, not even one of them voiced an opinion.

That experience blocked my career as an author until, two to three years later, a patient who was also a medium went into my office and asked, "Do you know who those two beings behind you are?" Slightly nervous, I looked behind me and, seeing nothing, told him that I didn't know. He immediately said, "They want to know why you have ignored them and haven't written your book." That gave me goosebumps since I felt an urgency to write my book for some weeks, and to cut off the conversation, I replied, "Why don't you ask them why they didn't write it while they were in the flesh?" On another occasion, another seer told me that my response disconnected us for a while, but that the time to do it was running out and that I still had their support. She prophesied that I would write a total of seven books in this lifetime.

The Outcome: The Book Is Born in a Weekend

I had already begun a routine of writing ideas and phrases that came to me in the early morning hours, which seemed not to correlate. The same thing happened at my office, and with phrases I shared on social media. You must know that, afterward, these phrases were incorporated as chapters or quotes to highlight messages in several of my books. The outcome took place when an astrologer and intuitive friend visited my office to treat pain in her limbs. Upon entering my office, when I tried to mention my book, she hushed me. She said: "Take it easy, I'm receiving a message from your Akashic records," and she went on to say that "they want you to adapt the original message or language into a simple format so that most people can understand it." She finished by saying: "It could be in 'bullet' format and with summaries that help clarify the message." That was the end of the conversation.

That weekend, I went to my office, sat down, and adapted the previous message into a humorous

273

school textbook format in two days. Integrating all that I had written one way or another helped ease the process. Thus my book trilogy on the school of life was born, which concludes with this volume. Approximately one year later, I intuitively perceived that I had to write a book that adapted the message for young minds in a cyber language that they can understand. I was surprised to find that I wrote this adaptation between seeing patients, during five working days, and when I finished it, I almost couldn't believe that I had written it. After nearly finishing the complete book editing process, I took a shower one day and, suddenly, had to get out and write the cyber version of the Lord's Prayer, which my editor was able to incorporate into the book.

I had an extraordinary experience during the development of this book. After visiting a jazz café with my wife, we met a lady for whom I felt a very particular affinity, who later turned out to be an intuitive astrologer. Walking to our cars while leaving the venue, she pointed out a lighted sign that seemed to spontaneously appear in one of the walls of a building (my wife never saw it), that the lady said was a message for me, and it was the word "Guardian." I tried to decode that enigma for several months until, one day, at a reading group meeting that dealt with extraterrestrial topics, I met a senior man who exuded wisdom and peace. I couldn't help sharing my previous experience. He smiled and told me: "You must read the Libros del Ser Uno (Books of Being One), and there you will find the answer to your enigma." And that's how I met the seer, Mrs. Franca Rosa Canónica, thanks to this marvelous book collection. These books have significantly influenced the development of my third book, which you just read.

Even though this book closes the school of life trilogy, if we believe the vision of one of the seers who was sent to enlighten me, it will not be the last book. There are still four books waiting to be written, to share the wisdom and knowledge I have been entrusted with spreading to the world. I hope you will come along with me on this journey.

BIBLIOGRAPHY

BOOKS THAT HELPED ME CREATE MY VISION, DIRECTLY OR INDIRECTLY

- The Bible

- Khenchen Palden Sherab Rinpoche: Door To Inconceivable Wisdom and Compassion

- Kenchen Palden Sherab Rinpoche: Opening to Our Primordial Nature

- Franca Canónico: El Ser Uno (6 volumes)

- Lao-Tzu: Tao Te Ching

- Rabbi Shimon bar Yojai: The Zohar

- The Three Initiates: The Kybalion:

- Paramahansa Yogananda: Autobiography of a Yogi

- Plato: The Dialogues

- Amit Goswami Ph.D.: The Self-Aware Universe

- Ken Wilder: A Brief History of Everything

- Chogyam Trungpa: Cutting Through Spiritual Materialism

- Scott Peck: The Road Less Traveled

- Hermann Hesse: Siddhartha

- Shantideva: The Guide to the Bodhisattva Way Of Life

- Sogyal Rinpoche: The Tibetan Book of Living and Dying

- Jerry Jampolsky: Love Is Letting Go of Fear

- Richard Bach: Illusions

- Dr. Henry Benson: The Relaxation Response

- Helen Schucman: A Course in Miracles

- Deepak Chopra: Quantum Healing

- Khalil Gibran: The Prophet

- Dr. Norman González Chacón: BioÉtica: La Medicina Natural, Una Alternativa Moderna

BIOGRAPHY

IVÁN FIGUEROA-OTERO, M.D. FACS, FAAMA

After graduating from the School of Medicine of the University of PR, Dr. Figueroa-Otero trains as General Surgeon at the University Hospital of the UPR, integrating a one-year fellowship in cancer and one in experimental research and clinic. Post-graduate studies in Pediatric Surgery at Miami Children's Hospital and the Hospital of San Juan Municipal Hospital followed.

Looking for non-surgical or less invasive options for pediatric conditions, Dr. Figueroa-Otero explores Eastern philosophies that emphasize a holistic concept. He was one of the first physicians to become certified in medical acupuncture in Puerto Rico, training in traditional Chinese medicine and acupuncture with professors from the University of Seville. Eventually, he was certified in medical acupuncture nationwide.

In 2009, the Doctor got a certification in anti-aging medicine. In December of that year, he retired from pediatric surgery, focusing instead on a comprehensive medical practice and emphasizing disease prevention and modifying styles life. In 2011 he was invited to become a Trustee of the American Board of Medical Acupuncture, which is the national body responsible for certifying physicians in the field of acupuncture through national exams. In that same year, he was recognized by Natural Awakenings Magazine as *Holistic Physician of the Year*.

Currently engaged in his private practice, Dr. Figueroa-Otero continues in his role as an educator, trying to achieve full integration of traditional Chinese acupuncture courses in the curriculum of medical schools, allowing the physicians to be certified both locally and nationally, and to establish clinical research protocols on the use of acupuncture in known conditions compared to the methodology established by modern medicine. Another immediate priority is to incorporate meditation techniques and their role in preventive and therapeutic medicine.

Dr. Figueroa-Otero is the author of the School of Life trilogy, with two previous books: Spirituality 101 For the Dropouts of the School of Life, and Spirituality 1.2 For the Disconnected from the School of Life. Both received awards from institutions like the Benjamin Franklin Award, NIEA Award, Readers Favorite, Beverly Hills Award, and USA Best Book Awards. They have also received excellent reviews by Focus on Women Magazine and the Kirkus Book Review, among others.

Made in the USA
Columbia, SC
02 March 2025

54575812R00163